I
Deserve Love

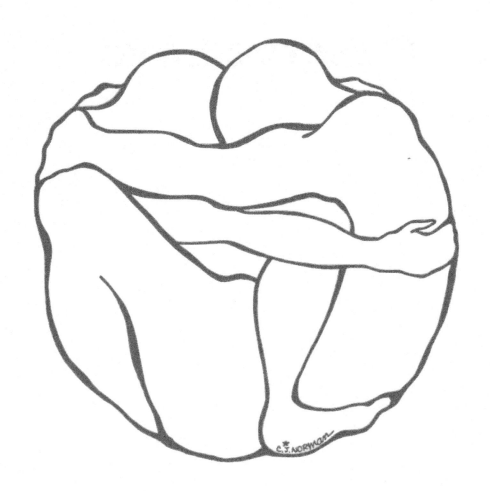

I
Deserve Love

How Affirmations Can Guide You to Sexual Fulfillment

By
Sondra Ray

Immortal Ray Productions

Nashville   Washington D.C.

IMMORTAL RAY PRODUCTIONS
301 TINGEY STREET, SE
WASHINGTON DC, 20003

Second Edition Publication, February 14, 2019

First Edition Printing, March 1976
Les Femmes Publishing
Millbrae, California 94030
Made in the United States of America

Library Of Congress Cataloging in Publication Data

Ray, Sondra
  I deserve love.

I. Success. 2. Conduct of life. 3. Sex
1. Title.
BJ1611.2.R38
131'.32
75-28774

First Edition
Celestial Arts, 1976
ISBN: 0-89087-909-5
12 13 14 IS 16 — 85 84 83 82 81

Second Edition
Immortal Ray Productions, 2019
ISBN: Paperback : 978-1-64516-736-5
ISBN: E-Book : 987-1-64516-737-2

Cover Design: Markus Ray
Cover Image: August Rodin's "The Kiss"
Back Cover Image: Judy Totton Photography of London.

I Dedicate this Book to:

Leonard Orr—my friend and teacher who taught me affirmations and influenced my life tremendously.

I also dedicate this book to my first publisher, Celestial Arts, who took a chance on me and published the first edition of this, my first book, *I Deserve Love*, back in 1975.

I mostly dedicate this book to my husband, Markus Ray, who is a conscious artist and poet—and his incarnation is his canvas. His life is a beneficial presence to all. He lives in solution consciousness and therefore always finds the solution to everything, including handling our life on the road. He also handles Immortal Ray Productions, our publishing wing, and breathes new life into our creative writing work. He lives the epitome of this book, *I Deserve Love*. It is wonderful to have your lover be your best friend. It is wonderful to have our love and passion also serving as a means to our greater spiritual development.

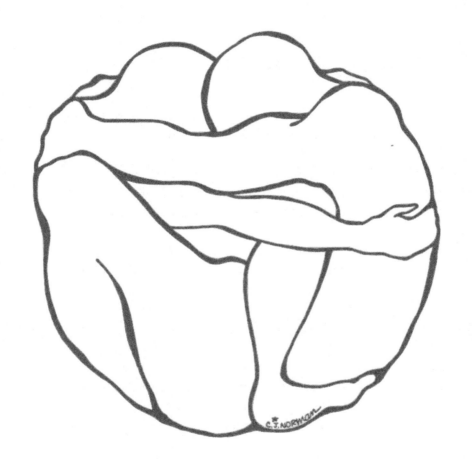

Table of Contents

Foreword

Back in the 1970's this book, *I Deserve Love,* by Sondra Ray changed the lives of a lot of people. It was her first book she ever wrote. This second edition, updated 40 years later, will probably do the same. It is honest and direct about sex in a way only Sondra Ray can be. It is celebratory of one of the most sacred functions of being human—sexuality. Although we have gone through the sexual revolution, and our own personal revolutions, there are still sexual issues people face in their everyday relationships. In spite of all the progress and openness we have achieved in this area of sexual fluency, relationships are still subject to all the issues we inherited from the past in our families, in our former relationships, and in the general challenges of just being human. Our minds still rule our sex life, and the thoughts behind a great and healthy sex life are still pertinent to these times.

When Sondra and I got together as a couple in 2008, after a 20 year period of going our separate and individual ways, we were clear about our purpose together. It was spiritual. Yet, within that spiritual function, a healthy sex-life was essential in my opinion. I said to her, "I'm not much into celibacy." My teacher, Tara Singh, was for the most part celibate for the last 30 years of his life. Maybe more. And this was not a spiritual imperative I embraced. In fact, I wanted to find in our relationship the ascendency of the spirit within the context of a healthy sex-life.

Just as intention and thoughts precede results, we have been able to find this Joy of Sex within the Holy Home of our Spiritual Life together. Rather than an opposition to spiritual advancement, sex is an enriching enhancement. And we wish this for other couples as well who have placed the "evolution of their souls" in the first place. A great sex-life can be part of that evolution, and *I Deserve Love* still offers a helpful set of guidelines to bring that sex-life into a more intimate and opulent flowering.

Sondra's "out of print books" are classics, and we still receive letters of how these old books have transformed people's lives. Recently a reader wrote:

> Hi Sondra,
> I stumbled upon your book "I Deserve Love" and really enjoyed it. I think it had a profound experience on how I think about life and wanted to say thanks for your meaningful work. —S.S. from Austin

Consequently, we have decided to get these old classics back in print, so people can "stumble upon them" a bit more easily. Sondra Ray continues to be prolific in her writing output on themes that are relevant to all ages.

I Deserve Love is the second in this series of 2nd edition reprints. The New Loving Relationships Book was the first. In reprinting these classics, and editing them for an up to date audience, I realized how universal these themes are to everybody. Sondra Ray addresses the basic issues facing us in nearly every aspect of living, and this is what makes her such a dynamic teacher and writer. She says not only what we want to hear, but what we need to hear. Facing our fears and dysfunctions is the first step in overcoming them—especially in the area of sex which is conventionally not discussed.

As I edited the material, I was astounded by the simplicity and directness of the affirmations Sondra wrote to correct just about any sexual dysfunction. We don't need Viagra and any number of chemical fixes to have a better sex-life free of problems—we need new thoughts about sex in ourselves and in our life. *I Deserve Love* offers these new thoughts. Helpful shifts of awareness come easily to Sondra Ray, and she shares them in this book in ways anybody can get it!

What could have been a problem before can now be a Joy and a pleasurable enhancement to your sex-life as a result of reading this book. What may have been suppressed and unexpressed can now be shouted from the rooftops with glee! Through applying the principles in this book, innocence reigns in an area that has conventionally been racked with guilt and psychic censorship. We are all out in the open now. *We Deserve Love*, and Sondra Ray's book is a catalyst for healthy sexual change in this 21st century, just as it was for us baby boomers of revolution in days gone by. Read it in faith and delight that your thoughts rule your life, and you can create the thoughts you want for a sex-life suitable to fulfill your every desire.

Markus Ray

Washington DC
January, 2019

Introduction

This is an updated version of my original first book, *I Deserve Love*, which I wrote in 1976, a few years after I became a Rebirther/ Breathworker in San Francisco. It introduces people to the use of affirmations, which back then was very revolutionary. I wrote these affirmations for clients who were having sexual problems. I had been trained as a sex therapist when I was a US Air Force nurse during the Vietnam era. I was stationed on a base in Arizona. During that time, patients who had their husbands on active combat duty needed a lot of counseling. So I convinced the Air Force to send me to California for some training in sex therapy. Way back then I did not understand the power of affirmations. But when I became a Rebirther/Breathworker, I realized that the problems the clients were having were in their mind. In other words, they had to change their minds in order to get things working properly in sex. I saved these affirmations and the clients themselves encouraged me to put them in a book. It was my first book. When I took it to a publisher they said that there were already too many sex books on the market. But, I argued, there has never been one dealing with the mind. I convinced the publisher and I am so glad I did. After that

I started writing more books and became a well-known author! Reading the affirmations out loud is helpful, but what is a lot more helpful is writing them over and over. You will know which ones apply to you. You can have fun with them!

Over 40 years after publishing *I Deserve Love*, using our mind to affect our life by harnessing the power of affirmations is just as relevant now as it was then. We still have not fully realized this power of the mind to affect change, nor have we fully examined the cause of our problems being held in our subconscious thoughts and memories. The effectiveness of the cure is in getting to the root of the problem—in all cases. It is not "New Age" rigmarole to say all experience is preceded by thoughts, and thoughts can be changed to render different results. And pardoning ourselves for these negative thoughts is taking full responsibility for our self-inflicted miseries. I discovered this Absolute Truth back when I began Rebirthing in 1974. It is still mind transforming when unequivocally applied. So here it is again, my main discovery, to ponder afresh in this updated second edition.

In the time leading up to this discovery my life went like this: I got my degree in nursing from the University of Florida in the early 1960's. Even back then I began to wonder if it wasn't backward of me to be passing out pills to sick people—some were dying—who really needed someone to prevent them from getting sick in the first place. I seemed to be at the wrong end. I finally dropped out, got married and we joined the Peace Corps.

After two years teaching health classes to Indian children in the high Andes of Peru, I somehow still found myself largely dissatisfied with my life. The next solution to my enigma seemed to be a Master's degree in public health. I ended up dealing with people in severe poverty and battered children cases. I was more depressed than ever. All the poor children I worked with were unwanted, or so I decided. I volunteered to work at Planned Parenthood. My marriage fell apart; that is when I joined the Air Force Nurse Corps to escape, or something.

I was assigned management of the obstetrics and gynecology clinic and became a nurse practitioner in family planning. I was delighted, at last, to be in the field of prevention. The women were so pleased to have a female practitioner that they poured out their souls to me, mostly about sex and marital relationships. Their husbands were in Vietnam flying combat missions. I saw what emotional pain they were in over these subjects and how, at the same time, pain was destroying their bodies with unnecessary illnesses. I began to study carefully how people could be free of sexual problems. I took every course then available to become a sex therapist. At the same time I began to explore the human potential movement.

I had a thought to go back to my X-husband, and I had all my things packed up and sent to Florida where he lived. But on the night before I was supposed to leave Arizona for Florida, I had a vision and heard a Voice—a full blown mystical experience—to go to California. "Never go back. Go to California," the Voice said. I heard it outside my head, and I know it was real because a friend of mine sitting with me on the floor of my empty apartment heard it too. He said, "Sondra, you better follow that Voice." I knew if I didn't I would regret it my whole life. So, I decided California was the place for me, and after only three days in San Francisco I found a job at a health center in Oakland.

In my first six months of living in California, I went through periods of rapid change as a result of my experiences in the human growth movement. I found a solution to a few personal problems which led to a revelation that changed my life. I had found myself in an unreal situation. I was wrecking my car every month, to the point that either I had to hire a chauffeur or stop driving. One evening I turned to two EST (the Werner Erhard course) graduates and told them I just didn't know what to do any more. I couldn't understand what was going on with me; I couldn't seem to get out of my destructive rut.

"Don't worry, Sondra," one of them said. "We'll take you to Leonard Orr." "Who is Leonard Orr?" I asked.

"Just come with us on Sunday," the other guy said.

I trusted them. At this point I was willing to try anything. In addition to my car accidents, I also had a pain in my body for thirteen years after my Father died, and my hair was falling out as a result of my divorce.

On Sunday we drove several miles into the woods of Portola Valley. And there was a beautiful rambling home and garden where about 40 people were gathered on the lawn. We stretched out in the sun and Leonard Orr began to talk. He wrote some things on a flip chart, and discussed the "five biggies" that sabotage our happiness. I knew immediately there was something very special about this man. His ideas turned my mind around, and I remember wishing I had had this information twenty-five years earlier.

I was so moved that I asked to see him privately. When we met he seemed very confident that I would be rid of my problems in no time. He not only introduced me to the use of affirmations, but also to his research on the Rebirthing/Breathwork process (in which I am presently deeply involved). At this point, Leonard gave me a couple of affirmations to write. I was doubtful and decided to test the theory.

"Do you mean to say that I could even get men to call me on the telephone using affirmations?"

"Of course," he said. "Try it."

What he told me to write was, "I now receive an abundant inflow of calls from men when I am at home." I had picked a hard one to test him. I had always had a certain nervousness about telephones which I related to my father's illness which began while he was an engineer with the telephone company. He died when I was a little girl, and so I concluded that telephones had something to do with death. I always managed to be "not home," or "just gone" when men called me—especially men whom I really cared about.

I wrote the affirmation Leonard gave me for about four days—ten or fifteen times a day. I couldn't believe what happened. All my old lovers called me—men I hadn't heard from for months, some for years. I decided then to see how far I could go with this affirmation, so I continued to write it for several days more. Incredible as it sounds, I began to receive telephone calls during the night, wrong numbers from men out in the world.

Somewhat embarrassed, I went back to Leonard, told him I had apparently overdone it and asked him to please help me reverse it. The new affirmation he gave me was, "I, Sondra, now receive telephone calls only from men I want to hear from." That worked, too. I was impressed. I was then willing to go ahead with the original affirmations he had given me. I wrote the following:

I, Sondra, now have a safe driving consciousness. My life urges are stronger than my death urges. As long as I weaken my death urges and strengthen my life urges, I will go on living in increasing health, happiness, usefulness, and youthfulness.

I have not wrecked my car since, nor have I experienced even the slightest hint of an accident. I also studied Rebirthing with Leonard Orr at the Theta House in San Francisco, and that launched my life in new and amazing directions.

I began to use affirmations in all areas of my life. I was most pleased about how well affirmations worked in my relationships. One of the simple affirmations that I most love to tell about is the one that helped me create my present relationship. I merely wrote this: "I, Sondra, am so happy and grateful my perfect mate is here now!" I met Markus, my perfect husband now for ten years, later in my life when most single women have given up.

After starting Rebirthing / Breathwork, all areas of my life now began to work so well that I saw clearly that I was getting closer and closer to my purpose. My health was perfect. I was hardly ever tired and I was constantly full of energy. If I did happen to get some minor ailment, I was able to cure it myself. I wanted somehow to figure out how to show others how to feel as good as I did.

Yet, I was hesitant at first to try affirmations with my patients at the health center, thinking that one had to be involved with metaphysics or have done something in the human potential movement to qualify.

One day I mentioned to Leonard that when I had new clients at the hospital, who needed sex therapy, I felt very drained and that I was having trouble getting my psychic energy together to handle it. He advised me that when this happened I should have the person write some affirmations immediately in order to deal with the negative mental mass and to change the psychic energy. At the time I felt this was a good idea, but I was still reluctant to try it. The day came, however, when I had three new clients in a row. I felt my body getting tense and very "heavy." Finally with the third woman I just pulled out a piece of paper and had the woman write:

I forgive my husband for hurting me.

She wrote it several times and I could actually feel the heaviness leave the room. She herself was relieved and began to get unstuck from the hatred she had been feeling for so long. She really did want to forgive him, anyway. From that day on I began to use affirmations with all the women I saw. They went away lighter, happier, and glad to have something tangible to use during the week. I began to write affirmations more and more freely on my own.

After I had worked with Leonard for some time, I asked him about the source of some of the things he had been teaching me. He told me I probably wouldn't believe him, but I urged him to share the story.

He told me about his teacher—a woman who had been born in Brazil blind, deaf, and dumb. She was "hauled around" by some nuns and somehow ended up at a leading medical facility in Minnesota where she was to undergo surgery.

Just before the surgeon began operating, she was visited by a spiritual guide whom she later came to call her "friend." This friend healed her, on the spot, totally. Instantly she gained her sight, hearing, and ability to talk. She did not need the surgery. The doctors fainted, and this incident is written up in medical books. Joël Teutsch was her name.

This woman then became the receptive student of her spiritual guide. Since she had never heard one word of negative conditioning, she had no reason to doubt or question anything the guide told her she could do. Therefore, she was able to perform all kinds of miraculous things, including bilocating her body. Leonard first met her at a metaphysical Bible interpretation class. When he heard her speak, he felt she embodied everything he had ever thought. He then studied with her for a number of years. Often her guide entered her body and taught her classes for her. Leonard also told me that whenever he needed her very much, she appeared to him. I experienced what he said as true, bizarre as it sounded.

Somehow it was enough of an answer to satisfy me. I did not question the theory of affirmations further, as it made sense to me that spiritual people would know and advocate the use of affirmations. After all, the writers of the Bible were inspired to write affirmations; the Bible is full of them and so are our psalms and hymns.

Since my first introduction to affirmations, I have adapted the technique to suit my own situations. I began to use the "Response Column"—so that I could see the emotional reactions people had and refine the affirmations to suit them more perfectly. But it is the affirmations that work, and what is important is that affirmations do work. Results are what count and results are what you can expect if you do affirmations properly. However, don't expect lasting results if you just read them or do them once or twice. If you have had a negative thought structure for years and years, it may take persistent attention to erase it—perhaps a month or so. The repetition of an affirmation for a month is less expensive than a year of psychotherapy.

It is important that you have a tool to change early negative decisions. That is what affirmations are all about and that is what this book is all about.

If you do not have loving relationships in your life, it is because you have negative thoughts that are blocking them. Why put up with crumbs when you could have the whole pie? You can give up your negative thoughts and change them to affirmations, and your whole love life will change. *I Deserve Love* is about making these changes. Even if you are in a pretty good relationship, you can make it even more awesome by reading this book—especially in the area of sex.

We had the new edition all but finished, then Markus said, "And what about the LGBT community? Don't they Deserve Love? How can we leave them out?" WOW. So here we are. I wrote another Part with four chapters called the Rainbow Millennium. Sexual preferences needed to be addressed, as well as Great Sex Over Sixty. And we needed a discussion on the various Erotic Accoutrements that are enhancing our sex life so plentifully in the 21st century. Last but not least, the LGBT community needed some attention. So we added a lot on these subjects that were not in the first edition of *I Deserve Love* forty years ago. We are now a Rainbow Culture, and our egalitarian ideals embrace a broader audience who deserves Love in the many different colors of the spectrum now available.

Love,

Sondra Ray

Part One

Affirmations

An affirmation is a positive thought that you consciously choose to immerse in your consciousness to produce a desired result.

Affirmations and Responses

I had a couple come to me with their sexual issues. Let's call them Susan and John. Susan was frigid, and we got down to the fact she had sex with her brother when she was growing up. She had so much guilt about it, it was hard for her to enjoy sex with John—or even have it!

John, on the other hand loved sex, but he had guilt as well—because he was a huge baby at birth, and felt he hurt his mother coming out. As a result, he was afraid to come inside Susan. And this was a problem, as they wanted to start a family.

To heal this I gave Susan this statement to repeat to herself, "I, Susan, deserve sexual pleasure." And I told her to observe her thoughts after saying the statement. These were her responses in bold:

"I, Susan, deserve sexual pleasure."
"I, Susan, deserve sexual pleasure."
"I, Susan, deserve sexual pleasure."....**No way!**
"I, Susan, deserve sexual pleasure."....**No—feel like crying.**
"I, Susan, deserve sexual pleasure."....**Impossible. I am bad, very bad.**
"I, Susan, deserve sexual pleasure."....**Need to be**

3

punished.
"I, Susan, deserve sexual pleasure."....*Dad will kill me.*
"I, Susan, deserve sexual pleasure."....*Never going to forgive myself.*
"I, Susan, deserve sexual pleasure."....*No that was too awful. Wrong to make love to brother.*
"I, Susan, deserve sexual pleasure.".... *No, I enjoyed it then. Dangerous!*
"I, Susan, deserve sexual pleasure."....*BULLSHIT!*
"I, Susan, deserve sexual pleasure."....*Can't see how.*
"I, Susan, deserve sexual pleasure."
"I, Susan, deserve sexual pleasure."....*Can 't imagine it.*
"I, Susan, deserve sexual pleasure."....*Who would want me?*
"I, Susan, deserve sexual pleasure."....*Don't deserve anything.*
"I, Susan, deserve sexual pleasure." ....*Is it possible?*
"I, Susan, deserve sexual pleasure."
"I, Susan, deserve sexual pleasure."....*Wow, that feels pretty good!*
"I, Susan, deserve sexual pleasure."

And for John, her mate, this was the statement I gave him to repeat, and his responses:

"It is okay for me, John, to ejaculate in a woman's vagina."....*Yea, right.*
"It is okay for me, John, to ejaculate in a woman's vagina."....*Maybe if that never happened.*
"It is okay for me, John, to ejaculate in a woman's vagina."....*I hate myself too much.*

4

"It is okay for me, John, to ejaculate in a woman's vagina."....*If I can ever get over hurting mom!*

"It is okay for me, John, to ejaculate in a woman's vagina."....*Well, could I get over that? (Can it be?)*

"It is okay for me, John, to ejaculate in a woman's vagina."....*Can I really? No, it can't be.*

"It is okay for me, John, to ejaculate in a woman's vagina."....*No, I am afraid it will hurt her.*

"It is okay for me, John, to ejaculate in a woman's vagina."....*No, I'll lose that warm, strong feeling in my penis.*

"It is okay for me, John, to ejaculate in a woman's vagina."....*I feel guilty because it is not right.*

"It is okay for me, John, to ejaculate in a woman's vagina."....*It's not right!*

"It is okay for me, John, to ejaculate in a woman's vagina."....*It is not okay because men are no good. I am ashamed to be a man.*

"It is okay for me, John, to ejaculate in a woman's vagina."....*I am afraid to surrender—don't feel safe in her—can't trust her.*

"It is okay for me, John, to ejaculate in a woman's vagina."....*Wish I could believe this.*

"It is okay for me, John, to ejaculate in a woman's vagina."....*Seems risky.*

"It is okay for me, John, to ejaculate in a woman's vagina."....*Confusion. feeling confusion.*

"It is okay for me, John, to ejaculate in a woman's vagina."....*Don't know.*

"It is okay for me, John, to ejaculate in a woman's vagina."....*Not yet.*

"It is okay for me, John to ejaculate in a woman's vagina."....*Maybe, someday.*

"It is okay for me, John, to ejaculate in a woman's vagina."....*Maybe. I think I can. I will try.*

What is going on here? These people are using a method we call using affirmations. It is very simple and, as you can see, it works very fast to get them in touch with the negative thoughts that were inhibiting their ability to enjoy sex. Using affirmations is more than just "positive thinking." It is a real catalyst for change because using them "brings up anything negative" standing in the way of manifesting your desired result.

The Power of Affirmations

The truth is that everything you need to know for a better sex life is within you. This book is the embodiment of a method that will make you aware of what is already in your subconscious and will tell you how to make it work for you immediately. All you need is a willingness to look at yourself and a pen and paper or a computer keyboard—whatever is most comfortable for you.

Many years ago when I worked as a sex therapist in a Planned Parenthood clinic in Arizona, I used the most up-to-date methods available at the time. Two years later when I was in the Air Force Nurse Corps I was able to produce good results with the same methods. The main problem was that those methods took so long, which was frustrating to my clients and to me. After I moved to northern California and became involved in some very powerful inner growth experiences, I gained invaluable insight into how people create problems for themselves and perpetuate them. The power to solve problems is in the mind, because the problems were made first by the mind. Since I have learned the Affirmation Technique and applied it in my work, every client has made rapid and significant changes—the kinds of results they could directly experience. They are using the power of their minds to make the changes they want, not only in their sex life, but in all areas of their life.

For example, until I began using affirmations with Susan and John, they verbalized only confusion and had no clear responses about what may have been blocking them. Susan came in telling me she couldn't enjoy sex and never had been able to. When she gave me her sexual history, there was no mention of an incestuous relationship with her brother. She had repressed it deeply and had no conscious recall of it. What she did talk to me about was her inability to allow herself any enjoyment.

John was able to masturbate to orgasm but could not ejaculate in a woman's vagina. He had tried other methods of therapy and had begun to get in touch with the cause, but was never able to change the result. He understood his fear of hurting women; but this did not help him to overcome the physical problem.

Using John as an example, you can see that all I did was help him to invert his original complaint—a negative thought that had become his seemingly "real" belief or *personal negative lie*—and make it a positive conviction by writing it as an affirmation, over and over. After three or four affirmations I asked him to hesitate after writing the next one to observe how his mind responded. Whatever resistance and objection his mind had to the affirmation was stimulated. I encouraged him to write down the responses on the right side of the paper. Each new thought or affirmation challenged his mind and at the same time made a new impression. The more he wrote the affirmation over and over, the less his mind objected. As you see by his last response, his mind was beginning to accept the new thought as his new reality within a very short time. He continued writing this ten or twenty times for several days. It then became obvious to both of us that as a little boy he had concluded that it was not good to be a man, based on what he had overheard his mother say about men, and he had built his reality around this negative connection. After reading his responses, I was then able to write more specific affirmations for him—he worked on such simple ones as "I, John, like being a man." He also put the affirmations on tape and played them before he went to sleep. After the first week he began to experience some changes. By the second week he could achieve orgasm inside a woman with only a little effort and emotional strain. The third week there was no problem at all, physically or emotionally.

After reading what Susan wrote as her responses, I decided to give her the following affirmation: "I, Susan, now forgive myself for having sex with my brother." She worked on it for a few days until she felt she had cleared out all her negative feelings in relation to the incident. She then began to see that she didn't have to keep punishing herself by denying sex altogether. Her outward circumstances changed radically as she began to like herself again. In a very short time, both of these people were able to do their own affirmations and accomplish their own sex therapy. They were able to experience directly the ways in which they were responsible for their own sexuality and how they could exercise conscious control over their minds to produce desired results.

As I continue to use the Affirmation Technique in therapy, I still am astonished by the quick results with so little effort. You, too, can do your own sex therapy in this way.

In the light of Susan and John's experience, I will reiterate: *An affirmation is a positive thought that you consciously choose to immerse in your consciousness to produce a desired result.* In other words, what you do is give your mind an idea on purpose. Your mind will certainly create whatever you want it to if you give it a chance. By repetition, you can feed your mind positive thoughts and achieve your desired goal. There are various ways to use affirmations.

Probably the simplest and most effective way that I have found is to write each affirmation ten or twenty times on a sheet of paper, leaving a space on the right-hand margin of the page for "responses," as John and Susan did. As the affirmation is written on the left side of the page, you also jot down whatever thoughts, considerations, beliefs, fears or emotions that may come into your mind on the right side of the page. Keep repeating the affirmation and observe how the responses on the right side change. A powerful affirmation will bring up all the negative thoughts and feelings stored deep in your consciousness and you will have the opportunity to discover what is standing between you and your goal. *The repetitive use of the affirmation will simultaneously make its impression on your mind and erase the old thought pattern, producing permanent desirable changes in your life!*

The truth is that thoughts produce results; and since realizations can very soon be discovered with this approach, the results are often startling. I would like to use my own life as an example. I struggled for years to alter my life-style and my circle of friends as well as my techniques in bed, thinking that these exterior manipulations would really improve the quality of my existence. I did learn much and I did grow a great deal; but somehow I always ended up with essentially the same results. I wondered why this was so since I seemed to be thinking new thoughts. I had become aware that positive thoughts produce positive results and negative thoughts produce negative results, so I tried thinking positively, of course. I still was unable to get out of some of my repetitive behavior patterns however. Positive thinking alone was not enough; there were two facts that I failed to understand:

- ❖ A person is the sum total of all his or her thoughts;
- ❖ Old thoughts continue to effect results even though one is no longer consciously thinking them.

In other words, my conscious mind had readjusted; but my subconscious mind had not. It seems that before the subconscious can change, a conflict must be worked through. If we have conditioned ourselves to feel that something is a "sin," and we want to do this "sin," we unconsciously feel we are breaking a "law." This conflict can be resolved by repeating the affirmation until the negative "law" (which is really a "lie") has been replaced in our subconscious mind.

In any case with the affirmations principle, I was able to uncover some negative decisions I had made very early in life. By changing those generalizations, I suddenly found myself released from the past. I gained the courage to begin doing the things I secretly had wanted to do. I became financially independent. I stopped having illnesses altogether. And I experienced relationships with men that are lasting, totally nourishing, and effortless. As you might imagine I became so excited over these changes that I could not wait to share them with my friends and eventually with my clients. I listened more carefully when people talked to me, and I began to notice their negative thoughts. Then I inverted those thoughts into positive ones and wrote affirmations for them by this means. I have not yet seen this technique fail on anyone who has used it.

After studying the power of the mind and the power of thought, I soon learned that all personal and sexual problems are grounded in negative thoughts. I could see that the method of induced autosuggestion utilized with affirmations was the obvious solution. Emile Coue used autosuggestion in his clinic in France at the turn of the century. He taught his patients to repeat "Day by day, in every way, I'm getting better and better." In fact, ancient liturgies are based on the affirmation idea—the ritual of the Catholic Mass is an example that exists today. The only problem is in the Mass you have to say, "I am not worthy to receive," before you receive the communion. Well, we have seen a lot of *Catholics* over the years stuck in the thought, "I am not worthy." It affects other areas of their lives as well. So the lesson here to learn about the power of creative thought: Watch what you put after, "I AM." It becomes instant manifestation until you change it in your subconscious mind.

Birth trauma is another phenomenon about which Leonard taught me and from which many negative thoughts and feelings can emerge. I went through the experience of unraveling my own birth trauma, and have since worked with clients on their birth traumas. From these *"rebirthing experiences"* I learn a great deal about a client's early decisions regarding sex which were made in infancy, or in some cases, even before that.

The so-called *rebirthing experience* happens in a breathwork session of deep, consciously connected breathing in the presence of a facilitator. After an extensive interview of exposing some of the deeper subconscious thoughts that are at the root of a person's issues, a period of consciously connected deep breathing help him/her release the charge of these thoughts from the Mind. Forgiveness and taking 100% responsibility for one's life results—and the thoughts that produced them—is coupled with a physical release on the cellular level brought about by the deep breathing. People clear their minds and bodies in Rebirthing, which we now call Liberation Breathing®. It is the fastest way to clear yourself of deep seeded patterns of debilitating subconscious beliefs and thoughts. After the breathing we formulate affirmations to help you practice getting the results and love you want.

Liberation Breathing can also be done in the water (using a nose plug and snorkel) in order to re-experience and remember your time in the womb and your birth. The process of reliving the experience is able to transform one's subconscious impression of birth from one of primal pain to one of pleasure. The effects of breathwork on a person's life are immediate: as negative energy patterns held in the mind and body start to dissolve; "youthing" replaces aging and life becomes more fun.

Recently one of my clients had a problem of feeling "pushed" by men as soon as the sex act was initiated. She liked sex and was orgasmic; however, she always had feelings of anger at the onset which she could never understand, nor could she seem to get them out of the way. I decided that it would be beneficial for her to experience "rebirthing." During her *rebirthing experience* her "hang-up" became very clear. Her mother's labor had been induced; and at the same time she, as a baby, was being pushed out fast, she was also being pushed back in the womb by the doctors because her shoulder had come out first. Her inner rage began then and there and had continued to affect her. Unconsciously she constantly set up situations for men to push her and then she would get angry at them—what she really was doing was trying to get even with the doctors.

I am not saying that everyone's birth trauma is the major factor in sexual difficulties, however, I do know that the birth trauma affects us daily. Some clients who were handled roughly during birth apparently decided the world is a hostile place and that they could not trust anyone. Others reached the conclusion that touching is awful. Some people picked up the desire of their parents for a child of a different sex right in the delivery room or womb, and their sexual identities have been confused ever since. The important thing is to have a way to change these early negative decisions and that is the role of affirmations. With them you can be your own therapist!

In Liberation Breathing Sessions we help people identify the thoughts they have that are giving them their results in life. You can book a session with us here and try it: **bit.ly/LBSession**. This of course means you can no longer be a *victim of circumstances beyond your control*, which you may not like. But it also means you have the Power of Affirmations to transform any situation you don't like by changing your thoughts, and building a new mindset with thoughts that will give you the peace, joy, happiness and *love you deserve!*

Making Affirmations Work for You

In Parts Two & Three you'll find affirmations covering many problems. Pick out those that apply to you and begin working with one by writing it five or six times. Continue to write it; after a time hesitate at the end for a response from your mind. When your mind responds, "okay," "true," or "accept," then you can be pretty sure that the thought is already working for you. However, if your mind responds, "no," "untrue," "reject," or the like, then you know you have resistance in that area. Look over the affirmations for which you have negative responses, and then choose the ones that you want to work with first.

As a reinforcement, you may want to write a few on small cards (one per card) and carry them in your pocket or in your purse. Glance at them while riding on a bus, waiting for someone, standing in line, whenever you have an opportunity.

Incidentally, after about a week of writing an affirmation or when you have gotten in touch with most of the negative responses your mind has to the affirmation, it is a good idea to stop using the response column (*your negative feelings and reactions*) and just keep writing the positive, affirming sentence. At this point you might want to switch to speaking them out loud as you record them on your mobile phone—then listen to them with ear phones. Recently I have also realized that it is just as effective for me to type affirmations—I am able to get ten written for each one I can do in longhand. Do what feels best for you.

Here is how to get the most out of the techniques of autosuggestion using affirmations:

1. Work with one or more every day. The best times are just before sleeping, before starting the day and especially whenever you feel "bummed out."
2. Write each affirmation ten or twenty times.
3. Say and write each affirmation to yourself in the first, second and third persons as follows:
   "*I, Sondra*, feel free to discuss all aspects of my sex life with my partner."
   "*You, Sondra*, feel free to discuss all aspects of your sex life with your partner."
   "*She, Sondra*, feels free to discuss all aspects of her sex life with her partner."
   Always remember to put your own name in the affirmation. Writing in the second and third person is also very important since your conditioning from others came to you in this manner.
4. Continue working with the affirmations daily until they become totally integrated in your consciousness. You will know this when your mind responds positively, and when you begin to experience the intended results. You will then experience mastery over your goals. You will be using your mind to serve you.
5. Record your affirmations on your iPhone and play them back when you can. I very often play them

while driving in the car on the freeway or when I go to bed. If I fall asleep while the earphones are still in my ears and the tape is going, the autosuggestion is still working as I sleep. (I am sure you are aware that I use affirmations in all areas of my life, for problems at work, problems with health, any problems at all. You can do the same.)

6. It is effective to look into the mirror and say the affirmations to yourself out loud. Keep saying them until you are able to see yourself with a relaxed, happy expression. Keep saying them until you eliminate all facial tension and grimaces.

7. Another method is to sit across from a partner, each of you in a straight back chair with your hands on your thighs and knees barely touching each other. Say the affirmation to your partner until you are comfortable doing it. Your partner can observe your body language carefully; if you squirm, fidget, or are unclear, you do not pass. He should not allow you to go on to another one until you say it very clearly without contrary body reactions and upsets. When he does pass you, go on to the next affirmation. He can also say them back to you, using the second person and your name. He should continue to say them to you until you can receive them well without embarrassment. This is harder than it sounds.

Another alternative at any time, of course, is to say them to yourself. You may not always feel like writing. However, writing is more powerful because more of the senses are involved.

So as you begin reading now, note which affirmations have the greatest emotional reaction or "charge" for you and mark them as you go. Try to have a good time discovering the secrets to your own consciousness. If you ever get to a point where you begin to feel upset, shaky, or afraid about something negative you learn about yourself, don't panic. Keep on writing the applicable affirmation over and over until your mind takes on the new thought. As it does, the negativity will be erased and you will feel lighter and better. Remember: It is just as easy to think positively as negatively. In fact it is easier. Negative thinking actually takes more effort.

Don't settle for so little in your life! You deserve a lot!

Beginning Affirmative Exercises

1. I,_____, was born with a limitless capacity for enjoyment and pleasure.
2. I,_____, have a basic trust that my affirmations will work and my efforts will be rewarded.
3. I,_____, am willing to move through my barriers of ignorance, fear, and anger so that my sexuality can assert itself.
4. Sexual satisfaction is a key element in my state of general health and well-being.
5. Every negative thought automatically triggers my creative mind into thinking three desirable positive thoughts.

These are really basic affirmations for your life and sexuality that will enable you to make them work for you. I suggest you do these first, in the manner described above, so you will get the most out of any future work we do in this book with affirmations geared toward your specific needs or issues. If you enter into this work with the thought "Affirmations don't work for me," then they won't. You have to begin with an open mind and a trust in the power of your thoughts to affect your life.

The Power of Ten Affirmations

In all the wet Liberation Breathing trainings we teach now around the world there is a practice we do with ten affirmations. The main part of it is this: find your 10 most negative thoughts; write them down, starting with your most negative thought you have about yourself (which we call your "personal lie"); turn all ten of these thoughts into positive affirmations; then memorize these affirmations. These become your new "life mantras" which start to turn your life around and enable you to feel better.

There is a power of ten, and a power you receive from memorizing the statements. It's as if your subconscious mind knows you are attentive enough to memorize the statements, and begins to take you seriously that you really want to change these negative thoughts and their results in your life. Trust me, this method really works.

Let's just say you are in a marriage and have two young children. You are staying at home taking care of the kids while your husband is out working in a job he really likes with a corporation that is *really* his cup of tea. He loves his work. He is so into his job he works long hours, and even comes home and the first thing he does is open up his laptop to finish stuff he was working on in the office. Dinner is getting cold and the kids are screaming, "Where's Daddy!" You are feeling ignored and unappreciated. You notice this is the same scenario from your childhood in which your Mom felt unworthy, undervalued, and unappreciated. Dad worked long hours as a regional sales rep for IBM, and did very well for the family, but was often "on the road." He had plenty of joie de vivre for his clients, but when he came home he just wanted to sit in front of the TV at night and veg out.

OK. Let's get down to it. Something has got to give here in this picture, but you don't know where to start. You notice you are recreating a similar scenario in your life, and copying your *mother's mind.* You are willing to take responsibility for making a change but are too angry about it to even bring it up. You are stuffing it just like your mother did. You think to yourself, "Well, the money is good, and I have a good lifestyle, but I feel like there is a major hole in my life." You spend all your time with the kids, and he spends most of his time with his fabulous career, and even your sex-life is fading into oblivion. Once a week has turned into once a month, and it's really bothering you. What to do?

OK, sit down and take control of your life, of your mind, and of the marriage you really want. Confess to yourself the problem by starting with writing down your ten most negative thoughts. Let's use Casey's story as an example. Here are her ten most negative thoughts:

1. I, Casey, am not worthy of love.
2. I, Casey, am not appreciated.
3. My husband has no time for me.
4. My life is too domestic.
5. We don't communicate in our marriage.
6. Sex is not flowing easily in our life.
7. I have to do everything alone.

8. I feel angry all the time but can't say it.
9. Some couples have great sex but not us.
10. I am wasting my life.

Now you have gotten it all out. THANK YOU for being so honest with yourself. Now let's look a little deeper into your dilemma. Usually you are "never upset for the reason you think, " so there may be some deeper thought factors and memories underneath your feelings of dissatisfaction.

Let's look at the thought "I am not worthy." That probably goes back a long while. Growing up Catholic, you had to go to church and say it a lot in front of the priest, "I am not worthy to receive." Mother also did not feel fulfilled in her life. She had low self-esteem and did not think she deserved to have her own dancing career that she put off when she started having you kids. She had a good figure, but over the years she gained some weight and started complaining her life felt empty.

You were a good student in school, but never felt worthy when you got A's on your projects. So most of the time you got B+'s. Dad was always working and you would remember waiting for him to come home so you could show him your English paper that got you an A-, the highest mark you ever had. When he finally saw it the next morning, all he could say was, "Next time I expect you to get an A+." Your heart sank and you felt unappreciated, no matter what you did. Dad had no time for you, and when he did have time all he gave was criticism.

Mom kept the house really neat and spic and span, but she spent most of her time doing that, and driving you kids around to school, and to after school sports and piano lessons. You never saw Mom and Dad talking about anything. You never even saw them hug or kiss or show affection. Dad just went to work, came home at night, watched some TV, and went to bed. Then the next morning he was out of the house early starting it all again. Mom was totally absorbed in the house and you kids. Not too many adults were in her life either. She did everything alone, it seemed.

One time Mom got really angry in the kitchen at breakfast and threw a towel across the room when your brother Jimmy complained that his eggs were too dry. She said, "You kids don't know what I go through. Nobody appreciates me!" You felt really bad for her, because deep down inside you really loved your Mom, and hated to see her so upset.

Now we are getting a clearer picture of why you are thinking the way you are thinking, and getting the results in your own life that you have. We tend to repeat what is familiar, even if it is not what we say we want, or what we think will make us happy. We repeat the family mind, or our mother's mind, or our father's mind. "The family mind is very intense," my teacher, Leonard Orr, would say. We tend to copy our parents' relationship to one another and to us, even if we did not like the way it felt to us growing up. The mind *seeks familiarity*. And we fall into the same pitfalls even if we say we never will. Our minds are conditioned by the minds of our parents and family.

What do we do now that we see we are just repeating old patterns? Well, we change the thoughts which created those results and patterns in the first place. So get out another sheet of paper and change those negative thoughts that are *programming your life* into a new program, by transforming them into new affirmations. They might look something like this, as in the story of Casey:

23

1. I, Casey, am worthy of love all the time.
2. I feel appreciated by those close to me.
3. My husband and I make time for each other.
4. I do interesting things outside the home.
5. I always speak my feelings to my husband.
6. Sex with my husband is now flowing.
7. I can receive joy doing things together.
8. I can express my activations without anger.
9. Having great sex is one of our priorities.
10. My life is always productive.

Memorize these statements. Even just reading them once will probably make you feel better, and give you more self-esteem. Memorizing the ten affirmations focuses your mind on a new reality for yourself, but you have to DO IT! What do you have to lose? Go on feeling stuck and miserable or take an action that will make a change and a difference.

The mind is more powerful than you think. And using your mind to make a change is something that has been given a lot of lip-service in all the New Thought circles, but requires actual practice and application to give you the miracles you want. You are in charge of your life, in the end. Your mind is a powerful catalyst for change, but you have to begin to harness it.

"I rule my mind, which I alone must rule," is Lesson #236 in A Course in Miracles (bit.ly/Lesson236). Are you going to claim your sovereignty? or go on feeling like a victim of your situation? The choice is yours to create your own heaven on earth in your life, or go along with the current status quo of some kind of polite hell. Which will it be? The power of ten affirmations will help you make this decision for a new heaven.

Part Two

I Deserve Love

Self-Esteem

Although all of my clients have benefited from affirmations, the one that strikes me as showing the best results in terms of self-esteem is that of Greg, aged 26.

When I first met Greg, he was living the life of a recluse in a one-room basement apartment. He was not working and he was not going out. He was afraid of social contacts—and especially terrified of women.

Greg had undergone a great deal of therapy before seeing me, so he was aware of the origin of his problems, but was still unable to get out of them to any degree. His feeling of self-hate was so strong that I started him out with the following affirmations:

❖ *I am more and more pleasing to myself every day.*
❖ *I am beginning to like myself as a man.*
❖ *I no longer have to hate myself as a man to please my mother.*
❖ *I am more and more lovable.*

Later on he was able to write, "I like myself; I am a lovable person." "Women are becoming interested in me," was another one. He put these on a recording to listen to them with earphones, in addition to writing them.

Now, one and one-half months later, Greg is moving out of the basement room, has returned to college, is getting a part-time job, and has a good, ongoing relationship with a young woman.

Self-Esteem Affirmations

I place these first because self-esteem really is the crucial element in an individual's capacity for sexual fulfillment or, indeed, fulfillment of any kind. If you work with these until they are assimilated, you will not only note the results quickly in your sexual life, but in all other areas of your life as well.

1. I, _____, am highly pleasing to myself.
2. I, _____, am highly pleasing to myself in the presence of other people.
3. I, _____, am learning to love myself more, every day.
4. I, _____, respect my own uniqueness.
5. It is more important that I, _____, please myself than to please men.
   It is more important that I, _____, please myself than to please women.
6. I, _____, am no longer dependent on a man's approval for my self-esteem.
   I, _____, am no longer dependent on a woman's approval for my self-esteem.
7. I, _____, like myself even if men are not present.

I, _____, like myself even if women are not present.

8. I, _____, deserve sexual pleasure.

9. I, _____, deserve sexual pleasure and so do other people.

10. I, _____, accept and acknowledge my individual tastes and pleasures in sex. (It is not necessary for me to enjoy what I think everyone else does.)

11. Because I, _____, like myself, I feel free to ask my partner to satisfy my individual sexual needs.

12. I, _____, have the right to ask for what I want in sex. I deserve all I can get—and so does my partner.

13. I, _____, am now good enough to satisfy myself all of the time.

14. I, _____, can trust myself and go at my own speed.

15. I, _____, am no longer helpless in sex.

16. I, _____, am self-determined and can play any role in sex I want to.

17. It is healthy to assert my right to pleasure during lovemaking.

18. My worth as an adequate male is not dependent on demonstrating my capacity for sexual conquest and potency. (Or—my worth and social status as a man do not depend on pleasing and seducing.)
My self-esteem as a woman is not primarily related to my capacity to arouse lust in men. (Or—my worth and social status as a woman does not depend on pleasing and seducing.)

19. I, _____, have the right to say no without losing my partner's love.

20. I, _____, have the right to say yes without losing my partner's love or my own self-esteem.
21. Any reaction I have during sex is totally okay.
22. Anything I feel like doing in sex is fine.
23. I, _____, am successful enough to please everyone.
24. I, _____, am good enough to please everyone and good enough to be satisfied by other people.
25. I, _____, am good enough to be loved by _____.
26. I, _____, am good enough to be satisfied by sex all the time.
27. It is okay for me to have a man/woman who totally satisfies me.
28. Men/women now eagerly want to have sex with me.
29. I, _____, now practice being good to myself.
30. I, _____, am not a failure. I, am a total success.

Love

Eileen, age 29, became totally possessive of the man whenever she fell in love and knew this had driven all her boyfriends away. She didn't know how to get out of it and always found herself sitting by the telephone waiting in agony. She had learned as a child to feel that possessiveness was a way to keep a man. At least she had concluded that by observing her mother, a very possessive woman whom Eileen had copied. Eileen had constantly had to compete to get the love of her father and since she never quite managed to do so, she became more and more like her mother in hopes that if she learned well enough she finally might get her father's love.

She acted this out with all men in her life, still trying to get the love of her father through each man. To make matters worse, her father beat her fairly often so she somehow had love hooked up with pain and tended to choose sadistic types for lovers, hoping to turn them into loving fathers, something she had never been able to do with her own father. Her distorted notions of love had been learned very early in life and she seemed unable to figure out how to love in any other way. After she had worked on self-love and self-esteem affirmations, I gave her the following:

- ❖ I, Eileen, do not need to be like my mother in order to win my father's love.
- ❖ I no longer set up other men to be my father.
- ❖ I deserve a man who loves me and treats me well.
- ❖ Love has nothing to do with pain.
- ❖ I am now willing to have a man who loves me.
- ❖ I forgive my father for not loving me in the past.

Eileen first began to clear up her relationship with her parents. She went home and tried to communicate to them exactly how she felt. Although they were not able to treat her much differently, she was able to begin to let go of the drama she had been recreating merely by expressing her feelings to them. She stopped hoping that she could finally change them and that they would meet her needs. Instead she began to meet her needs for love in more appropriate ways. She attended massage classes where she was finally able to work through her fear of being punished when men touched her. For her it was a gradual process of letting go of inappropriate behavior. Next she began to acquire male friends whom she learned to love as friends only. When she felt ready to risk a new kind of relationship, she listed all the qualities she wanted in a man and wrote her own affirmation:

- ❖ I, Eileen, can now attract a man who loves me and who is tender, kind, intelligent, open, affectionate, and easy-going.

She met him one week later.

Ultimately love is self-approval

Love is the place you are coming from, your ground of being. You are love.

Love is the divine force everywhere, the universal energy, the moving power of life that flows in your own heart.

Love is accepting someone as he or she is and as he or she is not.

Love is the acknowledgment of a union that already exists.

You already are part of this universal unifying essence called love. In addition, you are either loving or not loving. If you are loving, people will feel this attractive force and will appear in your path so you can love them. And there are multitudes of people who want to express their love to you. It is important to realize, however, that you cannot accept any more love than you are willing to give to yourself. Self-love—many people have had so much disapproval, they have forgotten how to go about loving themselves. What is self-love?

❖ *Self-love is acknowledging and praising yourself verbally to yourself.*
❖ *Self-love is approving of all your actions.*
❖ *Self-love is having confidence in your ability.*
❖ *Self-love is giving yourself pleasure without guilt.*
❖ *Self-love is loving your body and admiring your beauty.*
❖ *Self-love is giving yourself what you want and feeling you deserve it.*
❖ *Self-love is letting yourself win.*

- ❖ *Self-love is letting others in instead of submitting to loneliness.*
- ❖ *Self-love is following your own intuition.*
- ❖ *Self-love is making your own rules responsibly.*
- ❖ *Self-love is seeing your own perfection.*
- ❖ *Self-love is taking credit for what you did.*
- ❖ *Self-love is surrounding yourself with beauty.*
- ❖ *Self-love is letting yourself be rich and not staying in poverty.*
- ❖ *Self-love is creating an abundance of friends.*
- ❖ *Self-love is rewarding yourself; never punishing yourself.*
- ❖ *Self-love is trusting yourself.*
- ❖ *Self-love is nourishing yourself with good food and good ideas.*
- ❖ *Self-love is surrounding yourself with people who nourish you.*
- ❖ *Self-love is enjoying sex.*
- ❖ *Self-love is getting a massage frequently.*
- ❖ *Self-love is seeing yourself as equal to others.*
- ❖ *Self-love is forgiving yourself.*
- ❖ *Self-love is letting in affection.*
- ❖ *Self-love is authority over yourself; not giving it away to another.*
- ❖ *Self-love is developing your creative drives.*
- ❖ *Self-love is having fun all the time.*
- ❖ *Self-love is really talking to yourself gently and lovingly.*
- ❖ *Self-love is becoming your own approving inner parent.*
- ❖ *Self-love is turning all your negative thoughts into affirmations.*

You can start loving yourself this very minute and see how "high" you get. All you have to do is make up your own affirmations from the foregoing page. It's easy.

- ❖ I, _____, *now praise and acknowledge myself verbally to myself.*
- ❖ I, _____, *now approve of all my actions.*
- ❖ I, _____, *now have confidence in my ability.*

Write down other affirmations as you think of them. Notice how good you are starting to feel. The fact is, you are loving yourself as you write all the affirmations in this book.

So where is love? Nowhere is love not! Mostly it is there in the unfolding flower of your heart. I think you are getting the idea: it is better not to go searching outside yourself to find love. You must experience this self-love first before you can really experience anyone else's love. That is so important: You must experience self-love before you can experience anyone else's love. Already we are the ever sought wonderful thing we seek and seldom find. Finally, when you truly love yourself, your new problem will be how to handle all the love coming to you at once. And remember, love does not "run out." It is the moving power of life.

So how about you? Are you, or have you been, disappointed by love? Remember that you create your own experience with your mind. So if you have been creating everything that does not work in love, you can just as easily create everything that does work in love by the very same power. Just change your thoughts. Would you like to experience so much love that you would be in ecstasy all the time? Try loving unconditionally. Just try it. Would you like it if people were so attracted to you that they gravitated to you wherever you went? Would you like to give up having to search for love? Would you like to stop making such an effort? Would you like to have nothing but successful relationships? It really is easy. You are already on the way by doing these affirmations.

Loving Affirmations

1. I, _____, have love here inside me.
2. I do not need to struggle and drive for love. It is complete and absolute already.
3. I know love is here and as I, _____, am experiencing it, the search is over.
4. The sooner I experience my own self-love, the sooner I, _____, can experience the love of others.
5. I, _____, no longer deprive myself of the expression of love. I feel wonderful when I express love.
6. I, _____, do not hold back any of the love inside me. I express it, knowing that as I distribute it, I'll always be supplied with more.
7. The more I, _____, love myself, the more others love me.
8. The more I, _____, love others, the more others love me.
9. The more I, _____, love others, the more others love themselves.
10. The more others love themselves, the more they love me.
11. I, _____, daily make contributions to the aliveness and love of myself and others.

12. I, _____, am becoming passionately interested in everyone.

13. The more I, _____, participate, the more I am loved.

14. I, _____, do not resist love. I can let it flow in and out like water.

15. I, _____, radiate love to all persons and places and things I contact each day.

16. My purpose in life is to be loving and expanding and I, do this naturally and effortlessly.

17. People are just waiting to love me; not letting them do so is cheating them.

18. I, _____, am a free channel through which love always flows into expression. Nothing exists within me to block this flow.

19. I, _____, breathe in universal love and it enters through every pore and fills every cell of my body.

20. Love flows through me, _____, to all humanity.

21. I, _____, attract into my life now and always only loving, beautiful people.

22. I, _____, am a unique and priceless person, coming from a unique and perfect pattern hidden within me.

23. Others are inspired by the love I, _____, diffuse.

24. I, _____, deserve to be happy and I have the ability to rejoice in the happiness of others. (The more happy people I have around me, the happier I am.)

25. Everyone who tunes in to me from near or far is now receiving this message of love.

26. My love is instantly transmitted to the subconscious of another telepathically.

27. I, _____, do not allow myself to be affected by any ugly thoughts of worry, doubt, anxiety, fear, anger, or hate.

28. I, _____, instantly replace ugly thoughts with beautiful thoughts of love, peace, security, joy, confidence, happiness, and prosperity.

29. I, _____, am constantly turning negative thoughts into positive ones.

30. The love in me makes me forgive all and everything.

31. Love is my natural birthright. I, _____, claim it.

32. I, _____, am now a loving person worthy in all respects of having the kind of mate I desire.

33. As I, _____, send out this mental vibration of love, _____, will be drawn to me. (I do not need to scheme or to force this to happen.)

34. The more beautiful thoughts I, _____, have, the more beautiful loving friends and partners I will attract.

35. I, _____, am filled with this magnetic power so I draw to me the right type of loving relationship.

36. My true lover(s) are now being attracted to me.

37. I, _____, am an irresistible magnet filled with love. Love alone goes forth from me, and true love alone flows back to me.

38. I, _____, am love personified.

39. I, _____, am loving.

40. I, _____, am lovable.

41. I, _____, no longer stop the flow of love trying to come to me; I let it in.

42. I, _____, can draw to me the friends and lovers I have been waiting for.

43. I, _____, always deserve love. I deserve love for just being alive.

Loving Relationships

At one point in my life, I seemed to be in a pattern of attracting men who were very dominating, super-perfectionistic, critical, and exciting. I usually "set them up" as father figures, if they were not already. To complicate matters, I also set them up to leave me. This was because my father frequently left me to go to the hospital when I was little. One day he left me for good. My predominantly negative thought structures, generalized toward all men, were centered around the idea: "Men leave me."

Until I did affirmations I was unable to figure out how it was that men left me even though they seemed to really care for me. When I finally got fed up with all my neurotic relationships (that were not working), I decided I was ready to have a good relationship with someone very special. I did not feel like figuring out where to meet him nor did I feel like searching. I turned to affirmations and wrote "I, Sondra, am now willing to let into my life the kind of man I desire." (At that point in my life I was clear enough on the kind of man I did not desire anymore so I merely made a list of the qualities in a man I did desire.)

As I mentioned previously, I met my man I have now with the affirmation, "I, Sondra, am so happy and grateful my perfect mate is here now!" It took some determination and persistence, but it really paid off! We originally met years ago in the 1980's at a Loving Relationships Training; then we lost touch with each other for twenty years (while Markus was studying with his teacher of *A Course in Miracles*, Tara Singh); and then we met back up in 2008 at a Money Seminar I was teaching. At the very beginning of our relationship we both decided that we wanted a bond of deep ease and no-conflict. We have stuck with that decision. I also did most of the affirmations in this chapter. Our relationship has continued for ten years and has been completely nourishing and effortless to both of us.

If you have a good relationship with yourself, you will automatically have a good relationship with others. "The soul attracts that which it secretly harbors." In other words, you will attract the person who has harmony with your thought structures. If you feel really good about yourself, you'll attract someone who also feels good about him/her self. By the universal law of attraction someone will respond to the mental vibrations you exude.

You can create the perfect relationship for yourself by sitting down and listing the things you want in such a relationship. Meditate on them. Imagine already having such a relationship. Imagine the person you want for a partner. If you really are willing for it to happen, someone will come into your life just as you imagine, by this universal law of attraction. Thought creates vibrations which inevitably attract that which is in its image.

If you are already in a relationship, the same pro-cedure will work. Picture these positive, divine qualities coming out in him or her. Your partner will soon develop and become as you imagine. Jesus often spoke of the law of attraction. "As ye believe, so shall it be done unto you." "Unto him who hath, shall be given." When you come to understand that there is only one universal mind which is every place at the same time and in all things, you will see that the differences between you and others are illusionary. We are all just vibrating at different levels. Raise your vibration level and you will attract people on higher and higher levels.

Do not dwell on thoughts of the lack of things. There are no limitations. There is no lack in the universal mind (God) of which we are all part. Whatever you dare ask for you will be given. Watch yourself. Watch your thoughts. If you are thinking "I'll never meet somebody who etc.," you never will. Immediately invert the thought to something like this: "I am now attracting someone who _____ etc.

What you are willing to accept comes your way. Ken Keyes said "Happiness is experienced when your life gives you what you are willing to accept." So take responsibility for the thoughts you choose to think regarding relationships. Remember, we really are all related so you don't have to search and make effort. You can bring people you like into your life with your thoughts. The logical person to put into your circle is someone with whom you are in harmony—whomever you think you deserve.

Let's say you are now in a relationship. You may wonder how to make or keep it successful. It's easy. A successful relationship is based upon one being nourished by the other person's presence. That is enough. You don't have to do anything else except set up certain agreements; make it a game. Don't get stuck in the rules, however. You might want to change them as frequently as every week. All you have to do is negotiate.

It is important to remember that you must experience your own self-love before you can experience another's. A loving relationship is when two people experience each other's being. In a loving relationship, the loving is absolute already. It is in the "relationship" that the action comes in.

Loving relationships can benefit you immensely. (So don't deprive yourself.) Another person can enrich you. Another person can assist you to grow faster. Another person can enlighten you, fast. Your negative patterns are likely to come up quickly for you to see. Since you attract what you are, you have a mirror at all times to see yourself. Your partner can be your personal Guru. You always get value.

Loving Relationship Affirmations

1. I, _____, am no longer looking for the right person. I am becoming the right person.
2. I, _____, am a responsible person who is happy and free with or without a mate. I can survive equally well with or without a man or woman.
3. I, _____, learn to please myself, I can have more mutual and honest relationships.
4. I, _____, am a full person, capable of an open, loving relationship.
5. As I, _____, think more positively, I will attract positive thinking people into my life with whom I can have nourishing relationships.
6. I, _____, am now attracting into my life someone who is loving and pleasurable.
7. I, _____, have a lot of love inside me that flows outward easily thus making me even more able to love.
8. I, _____, am able to handle an intimate, warm, affectionate and close relationship.

9. I, _____, am now able to intuitively experience the being of another.

10. I, _____, no longer need _____ for my survival and _____ no longer needs me. _____ now loves me and enriches my aliveness and I, _____, love _____ and I am enriching his or her aliveness.

11. I, _____, think highly of myself and therefore it is easy for me to accept _____ thinking highly of me.

12. I, _____ , am careful to state the type of relationship I want rather than how _____ should change.

13. It is okay to disapprove of my partner's actions as long as I am not disapproving of his being.

14. I, _____, am careful to state my feelings rather than judge _____ and his feelings.

15. I, _____, am equal to my partner(s) and he or she (they) is/ are equal to me.

16. There is an abundance of lovers who are just right for me.

17. I, _____, no longer experience anxiety about the loss of those people who really count in my life. My love objects have permanence.

18. I, _____, now feel secure about the dependability of my relationships.

19. My relationships last as long as I want them to.

20. The satisfactory ending of a relationship frees me to enjoy other refreshing new ones.

21. I, _____, am now developing loving, harmonious, and lasting relationships with men.

I, _____, am now developing loving, harmonious, and lasting relationships with women.

22. I, _____, now have a success consciousness with all my intimate relationships.

23. I, _____, am already related to everyone in the universe so I do not have to "work at" forming relationships.

24. I, _____, can easily have relationships for the purpose of recreation.

25. I, _____, no longer resent people coming into my space because they love me.

26. I, _____, get value out of every relationship because I use it for expansion and enlightenment.

Loneliness

Joan and her husband were barely on speaking terms. They were unclear if they even wanted to stay together. However, Joan kept hanging on because she was afraid to be alone. It became obvious that what was needed was a separation so that each could sift through his and her own feelings. Her husband was willing. Joan did not think she could make it alone. However, they did separate. Joan began working on affirmations and began to read self-improvement books. She found she actually began to enjoy her time alone and used it to get herself together. She felt happy that she was much stronger as a person than she thought. She started to "date" her husband again, and talked about the feelings that had come to her consciousness while alone. Because of her new positive attitude the separation worked and after one month they reunited and began a whole new relationship. They celebrated by taking a cruise to Alaska for a second honeymoon.

Being alone is simply the state of being without others. However, loneliness is often defined as a state of sadness and anxiety from want of company—that is only one response to being alone. Fear of loneliness is only one response to being alone. Fear of loneliness is often related to fear of suppressed feelings. These feelings may appear too great to confront when one is in a helpless state or a "victim" state. Actually, it can be extremely valuable to let suppressed feelings come to the surface. For example, if a person can analyze these feelings and see what holds him back in life, it can obviously be an enlightening experience. Loneliness can be a time of self-discovery and self-renewal if one can see the possibility for such growth.

As Tillich put it, "Loneliness is a word to express the pain of being alone . . . and solitude is a word to express the glory of being alone." To turn loneliness into solitude requires self-approval and the awareness that being alone is not a loss or a punishment, but is in fact an opportunity to gain new certainty about one's self. The fear and pain of suppressed feelings passes quickly when one is willing to discover the truth about those feelings.

Are you lonely? Did you become that way through a separation, an experience of rejection, or from feelings of guilt? Does the situation seem hopeless? There is a way out and the way out is through solitude, even though it may not at first seem so. If you can take responsibility for where you are and for the circumstances which got you there (without punishing yourself), then you can feel in control of the situation and use it to serve you. The truth is that your relationship with others is based on your relationship with yourself. Being alone is being in that primary relationship without interference. Being alone is a perfect opportunity to begin to love yourself. Loving yourself and using your power constructively will allow you to create the kind of relationship you want with others.

Loneliness Affirmations

1. I, _____, realize solitude is an opportunity for me to develop my self-esteem.
2. The more successfully I, _____, handle solitude, the more successfully I'll handle my relationships.
3. The better I, _____, know myself, the better I can communicate.
4. The more I, _____, enjoy being alone, the more I can enjoy being with people.
5. Since there is no one exactly like me, I, _____, am interesting to myself.
6. I, _____, realize being alone enables me to make decisions.
7. When I, _____, am alone, the potential for my real feelings is aroused; and this is valuable to me.
8. I, _____, am now willing to let my suppressed feelings come up to the surface and to discover new insights about myself.
9. I, _____, find even depression gives me the opportunity to discover something about myself.
10. When I, _____, am alone, I have a wonderful opportunity to meditate and gain peace of mind.
11. I, _____, can achieve self-awareness through solitude.
12. My creativity is enhanced when I am alone.
13. I, _____, realize solitude is an opportunity for me to experience my intuitive connection to infinite intelligence.
14. I, _____, can now be alone as much as I want to.

15. I, _____, can stop being alone anytime I want to.

(Remember, you are what you are searching for.)

Jealousy

Tony and Maureen were having more and more arguments about his outside relationships. Maureen was having continual emotional outbursts and crying spells, while Tony was getting less and less discreet about his affairs. Maureen wanted a monogamous relationship, she claimed, and yet she had not attempted to look for someone else who was also interested in monogamy. Tony claimed he wanted sexual freedom and a woman who could handle that, and yet he had not tried to find a woman who could. After exploring the "payoff' that each was getting, it appeared that Tony had purposely found a way to get Maureen's disapproval. He was used to disapproval from his mother, so this kept "the game" going. He was also used to a very emotional, volatile kind of communication from his mother. And since Maureen was a quiet person, his maneuvers were a way to get a rise out of Maureen—a method to get her to emote on the level he had been previously used to.

Maureen's part in her game was that of having felt second place in her father's love. As an only daughter she was very attracted to her father and constantly jealous that her mother "had him." Therefore, she acted out the competition she had felt for her father's love in her relationship with Tony, (who was quite a lot older than she, and similar in looks to her father). I suggested to Maureen that she start approving of Tony's behavior so he no longer had a payoff, and that she begin to "work through" her suppressed incest. I suggested to Tony that he start to be responsible in his use of outside relationships. After the consultation, things appeared to be worse; the truth was out and a blow-up ensued. Tony and Maureen separated. However, in a few days, each called me individually asking for help in changing their patterns. I gave them the following affirmations.

I, Maureen, now approve of Tony and take the responsibility for my feelings of jealousy.

The more freedom I give Tony the more he loves me.

Since I no longer need Tony for my survival it does not matter if he has other Partners.

I, Maureen, no longer need to see Tony as my father and struggle to get his love.

I, Maureen, am now willing to let my incestuous feelings toward my father surface.

I, Tony, now take the responsibility to establish agreements about outside relationships.

I, Tony, am careful not to use outside relationships as a form of manipulation.

I, Tony, no longer need to set up Maureen as my mother.

I, Tony, now let Maureen communicate openly in a harmonious way. I no longer need the dramatic outbursts I was used to as a child.

Since Maureen had no guarantee that Tony would be faithful, she agreed to work on the first affirmations I gave her in order to handle it better and take the pressure off of him. When Tony saw her approving manner, he could not believe it. He was very confused at first because he could not handle getting the approval he thought he wanted. The game was over for him—the old payoff was no longer there. In spite of this he did not stop trying to work things out. Just getting in touch with his underlying purposes in the game helped him eventually to give it up. Maureen also began to work out her incestuous feelings by analyzing her dreams and found that very releasing. She took a more mature approach to the relationship and both agreed to have an option for outside relationships on a very limited basis.

Jealousy Is Not Love

Love is not jealousy.
Love is not need.
Love is not ownership.
Love is not hoarding.
Love is not clinging.
Love is not restricting.
Love is not prohibiting.
Love is not bondage.
Love is not slavery.
Love is not dependency.
Love is not possession.

Jealousy is *not* love.
Imagine a world without jealousy.

Imagine being able to be with whomever you wanted to whenever you wanted to and having your mate be pleased about that.

Imagine feeling really good about seeing your partner with someone else.

Imagine even getting thrilled over his being able to have pleasure elsewhere, as well as with you.

Imagine feeling really high sharing your partner with someone else.

Imagine your partner feeling really high sharing you.

Imagine having no fear at all of being replaced by that other person.

Imagine never having to worry about being alone.

Imagine everyone spreading love around with no guilt.

Imagine everyone being glad to see his or her lover spread more love around.

Imagine a powerful attractive force going so strong that everybody got enough love.

Many people who are totally on the other side of jealousy feel as if they are in Heaven. They are not necessarily polygamous at all. They may still prefer complete monogamy. But they have the *choice*. They have the *option*. And they love this freedom. Jealousy, a present-time fear of a future-time loss, manifests itself in one or many of the following ways: demand for exclusive attention, distrust, criticism, obstinacy, urge to get even, self-destruction, restricting another's freedom, and stopping another's pleasure. Jealousy is often considered an innate feeling; however, a more careful look reveals it to be an unconsciously acquired tool for the enslavement of another. It can usually be traced to childhood in which there was a feeling of being neglected or discriminated against. It is a good idea to know that what we often are upset about is not really what we are upset about at all. We are usually re-experiencing feelings of primal pain, and yet your partner cannot compensate for or replace your parent's love.

Since most of us have been prepared by our parents for an exclusive one-to-one relationship when we grow up, we expect this single relationship to provide complete comfort and satisfaction. However, this kind of relationship, which can often become addictive, is usually false security. This is especially so when the dependency is heavy and one needs more and more doses to feel happy.

If your happiness depends on another you are likely to be in trouble. If you keep thinking love comes from outside yourself, you will constantly fear being alone, fear losing your mate, fear he will spend too much time away from you. And then there is the danger that you will cause these things to happen by a self- fulfilling prophesy. Negative thoughts are creative. In other words, you can love another without fear or anxiety if your self-worth is not dependent on him or her. Affirming your own self-worth to yourself helps free you from your fears and allows your partner to love you even more.

I think that you intuitively know that where jealousy exists real love is thwarted. I think you also know that you don't have to suddenly give up monogamy to get over jealousy. And I think you probably know what works. What works is continually raising your self-esteem and making agreements with your partner. What seems to work best is making an agreement with your partner that you are both willing to keep, at least until you feel you want to do something else. Then you merely have to negotiate new agreements.

The main thing is a commitment to make the primary relationship work. Then one only needs to ask in regards to having an outside relationship, is it *supporting* my relationship? If people would choose to have an open relationship only after answering that question with a positive answer, and then "clear" themselves with the affirmations for handling an open relationship, there would be much less chance of destroying the relationship. If you cannot answer that question positively, and go ahead anyway, you are treading in dangerous territory.

If you still feel jealous, acknowledge that that is "where you are at"; and set out to raise your self-esteem. Don't berate yourself about it. Meanwhile, here are some affirmations you can try.

Jealousy Affirmations

IN OUTSIDE RELATIONSHIPS

1. I, _____, now take the responsibility to establish agreements with my partner about outside relationships.
2. I, _____, now take the responsibility for my feelings of jealousy and no longer blame it on my partner.
3. The more I, _____, win, the better I feel about others winning; and the more others win, the more I win. Therefore, I win all the time.
4. The less dependent I, _____, am, the more love I get.
5. The more freedom I, _____, give my partner, the more he or she loves me.

6. The less I, _____, need my partner, the more he or she loves me.

7. I, _____, am now willing to let my partner establish other relationships and I give myself the same right.

8. When I, _____, have outside relationships, I do it with a clear conscience so that guilt docs not become an interference.

9. I, _____, want my partner to have the same peace of mind in outside relationships.

10. I, _____, am careful not to use outside relationships as a form of manipulation. (I am aware of my purpose and take responsibility in the matter.)

11. Since I, _____, no longer need _____ for my survival, it does not matter if others are involved with him or her.

12. The more my partner is with others, the more interesting and stimulating he or she is to me.

13. I, _____, welcome anything that adds to the richness of my partner's experience.

14. When my partner and I are loving each other, it makes more love for another.

15. When _____ is loving _____, I feel more loved by both. It is making more love for me.

16. When I, _____, share the people I love, the more love there is to go around and the more I get.

17. The more people I, _____, give my love to, the more love I have, and the happier my partner is.

18. The excellence of another can only contribute to my mate.

19. It is okay for me to have the desire to expand myself through other relationships.
20. My lovers now approve of each other.
21. My mother approves of my sex life.
22. My father approves of my sex live.
23. My minister approves of my sex life.
24. God approves of my sex life. Christ intended for me to have abundance.
25. I, _____, approve of myself whether I have more than one lover or not.
26. I, _____, have the right to have multiple sex partners.
27. Since I am divine, I have choice and I am willing to take the responsibility for my own choices.

(Love is like a magic penny. The more you give it away, the more you get back.)

FOR THOSE WHO WANT AN EXCLUSIVE RELATIONSHIP

1. I, _____, approve of myself whether I have just one lover or not.
2. It is okay if I, _____ , choose to be monogamous. I trust my decisions.
3. I, _____, now choose to have an exclusive relationship and I am free to change my mind at any time.
4. My relationship with _____ is growing fuller and more satisfying every day.
5. I, _____, no longer have to prove anything by having more than one relationship.
6. I, _____, no longer want to get even with my partner by having outside relationships.

7. I, _____, can be totally nourished and satisfied by one person.
8. I, _____, now recognize that my partner, _____, can satisfy all my needs.
9. My sex life with _____ is growing more satisfying daily.
10. I know that what I choose is right for me and I do not judge others for their choices.

Part Three

I Deserve Sexual Pleasure

The Value of Sex

A 25-year-old married woman called Ming came to me complaining of disliking sex and not knowing why. She felt it had something to do with her parents' strictness, but she could not recall ever having been told anything negative about sex. Rather than spend session after session uncovering all of her past, I had her begin immediately writing very simple affirmations such as *Sex is natural, Sex is for pleasure and fun*, among others. Her most dominant negative thought structure surfaced quickly in her responses. It had to do with sex being a "duty," and since she was a naturally rebellious type she therefore rejected sex altogether.

The response column also revealed that she still had some feelings that sex was only for having children, even though she thought that she had already let go of that part of her early conditioning—intellectually she had, emotionally she had not. She did most of the affirmations in this chapter, and, fortunately, was willing to share her writing with her husband. He became very interested in the new things he was learning about her and decided he wanted to come to see me too, in order to assist her in the changes she was trying to make. He began to express the suppressed resentment he had toward her and told me that they had been on the verge of a divorce over their sexual relations. For a time they separated but both continued to do the affirmations I had given them including those on self-esteem and loving relationships. After a short while they reconciled, and Ming has been able to look at sex in an entirely new and natural way.

It really doesn't matter if you consider yourself part of the liberal "new sexuality" or if you prefer to maintain more traditional notions about sex, you still may have the idea that sex is "bad" without realizing it. Many of my clients who had professed to have positive beliefs about sex were really still operating from old negative beliefs. As long as these old thought patterns are still present in your subconscious, they will limit your willingness and ability to experience and express your full sexuality. If you are thinking new liberating thoughts about sex and still getting poor results, it may be that your old thought structures are still dominating you even though you no longer consciously think them. You may find many surprises about yourself in this area as you write the sex affirmations and observe your responses.

Although it seems clear the primary purpose of sex is pleasure, there is, of course, also the possibility of having children. The old paradigm was that sex is for procreation—and pleasure, especially for women, was not that important. I continually talk to women and men who have adopted the new thought of wanting no children or, perhaps one child, but somehow they have not realized the necessity of adopting the other new thought that *must* go with it: responsible birth control. Or perhaps they realize the importance of birth control but still have retained old thoughts that they are worthless as people unless they conceive and, therefore, purposely but subconsciously "forget" to use birth control. The drastic alternative of repeated abortions does not seem to enhance the pleasure value in sex. If you really do not want children, responsible contraception is a must for a good sex life.

Sex Affirmations

1. I, _____, realize sex is natural.
2. I, _____, know sex is fun.
3. I, _____, know it is okay to enjoy sex.
4. I, _____, know sex is for pleasure.
5. Sex has a beneficial effect on my relationship with _____.
6. As I, _____, deal more honestly with my sexuality, I free up lots of energy for satisfying work, play activity, and living.
7. I, _____, no longer have to pressure myself to perform in sex. I can see it as recreation.
8. I, _____, feel the sexual act is an act of aliveness and unity.
9. Sexual expression always makes me feel more alive and fulfilled.
10. I, _____, am not just a passive instrument used for my partner's pleasure. I am self-determined about gaining my own satisfaction.
11. I, _____, can be an "enjoyer" rather than an "observer" or "performer."
12. The more I, _____ , make love, the better lover I become.
13. The more sex I, _____, have, the better I feel.
14. It is okay for me to enjoy sexual pleasure responsibly without conceiving children; or, I,

_____, am glad that I always menstruate regularly.

15. My worth as an individual does not depend on conceiving children.

16. I, _____, have a right to use contraceptives of any kind.

17. I, _____, am responsible about using appropriate contraceptives.

18. I, _____, find that once this responsibility has been fulfilled, I can relax more.

19. The more I, _____, allow myself sexual pleasure, the more youth, energy, beauty, and love I gain.

20. Sexual pleasure is a virtue.

21. The more sex I, _____, have, the more spiritual I become.

22. I, _____, no longer fear being resented for having a good time in sex.

Sexual Desire

Sheila, a divorcee in her 30's, had been experiencing difficulty getting turned on with her most recent lover. She had no similar trouble with her ex-husband, even though it had been a stormy relationship. Nor had she had any trouble with other lovers since her divorce. What disturbed her most was that she was now in a very exciting relationship with a younger man (we'll call "Bart") whom she found very sexy and to whom she was very attracted. On the surface it appeared that it was a simple problem of age difference as a barrier. However, both of us felt there was more to it. When she wrote, "A man's age does not affect my sexual desire," her responses were always positive. However, when she wrote, "I am easily turned on and filled with desire when I am with Bart," the responses were more revealing. They were in the following vein: "No, he does not provide for me." "Sex has to be earned." "Why should I be interested when he doesn't have any money?"

Sheila was surprised to learn that she had somehow hooked up sex and money. She admitted that all the men she had slept with in the past had provided for her financially. She was very interested in clearing this matter up, since she loved this man and chose to stay with him even though he did not support her financially. The affirmations I gave her were as follows:

I desire sex for the pleasure I derive from it.
Sex has nothing to do with money.
I can support myself.

She really did want to financially support herself but Bart gave her the emotional support she needed: Interestingly, he was not angry with her when she communicated the truth to him and the relationship worked out very well.

Webster defines desire as: To long for, crave; to ask for; also as sexual appetite. A lot of us will allow ourselves to indulge our desire for new cars, houses, clothes, boats, and any other material thing, but will deny ourselves the simpler, more lasting, and certainly less expensive pleasures that are readily available. I see many people who simply won't allow themselves sexual pleasure because of their low self-esteem, because of self-hate, desire for punishment, or misplaced values. These people don't often even get up to the level of real sexual desire. They simply shut the whole thing off.

In addition, I have often seen cases where one person waits for the other to instigate sex so that he or she can always say, "I wasn't responsible. I couldn't help it." This is a way to avoid admitting that they like sex, which is something that is hard to do if you still have the thought structure that sex is somehow wrong. Clearing your head of the negative responses that come forth as you affirm your sexual appetite will free you to express your desire.

Even though this section overlaps with body sensations and the value of sex, I suggest you check your desire level by responding to each affirmation truthfully and working with those which give you the most trouble.

Sexual Desire Affirmations

1. I, _____, am interested in sex.
2. I, _____, give myself permission to enjoy sex.
3. I, _____, no longer feel restrained . . . I now allow myself to be filled with desire.
4. I, _____, am now fully aware of my desires.
5. I, _____, desire sex for the pleasure I derive from it.
6. It is okay for me to acknowledge my need for sex.
7. My sexual drive is increasing.
8. In fact, every day my erotic appetite is increasing.
9. I, _____, am willing to express my sexual desires.
10. I, _____, am now filled with a healthy sexual appetite and desire.
11. I, _____, now take the responsibility for being interested in sex.

Fantasies

Jack, age 25, fantasized a lot about men when he was having sex with his female partner. He was not only terrified by fears of homosexuality because of this, he also was concerned that it meant he didn't really love the woman and made him feel disloyal. When he wrote, "I no longer have to fantasize about men," he experienced anxiety just writing the affirmation. I encouraged him to stay with it and to write down all the fears that came up to his consciousness as responses. The two predominant factors that emerged were wanting his father's love and, more strongly, the underlying fear that he might not be able to perform with a woman. The fantasies about men kept him from being "here now" and from having to confront these two things. Writing out his fears helped him to face them better than if I had merely pointed them out to him. He could not deny them since he wrote them himself and, in fact, was relieved to find it wasn't as bad as he had expected. I helped him construct his own affirmations which turned out as follows:

> I no longer have to fantasize in order to get my father's love.
> I do not have to perform for women any longer.

I can experience my own pleasure in sex.

He had always been extremely afraid to tell anyone about his fantasies, especially his partner. But after he learned the reason for the fantasy he felt free to share this information with her. He experienced great relief in telling her and told me that he couldn't believe how fulfilling it was to actually be "there," present in the love-making experience, without pretending he was somewhere else.

Your sexual fantasies surely have a very personal meaning to you. They are fine as long as they are not a distraction from experiencing the pleasure that is going on. Try using them in a creative process to get a lot of clues about yourself and your inner thoughts. Let your fantasies serve you.

Affirmations About Fantasies

1. I, _____, am okay whether I fantasize during sex or not.
2. I, _____, no longer have to fantasize to arouse myself or experience desire.
3. I, _____, can be aroused with or without fantasies.
4. I, _____, have new freedom to enjoy my fantasies, to learn from them and accept myself as I am.
5. It is healthy to tell my fantasies and share my feelings about them.
6. I, _____, feel free to explore all parts of me that might come up in fantasy, daydreams and dreams at night.

7. My sexual fantasies are not abnormal. They are perfectly normal.
8. I, _____, am not disloyal to my partner if I fantasize.
9. Fantasizing while having sex is normal, healthy, creative and honorable.

Body Image

A case history I remember very well was that of a 25 year-old girl named Katy who told me her sex life was no good because she was too embarrassed about her body. Katy was overweight and had tried numerous diets, all of which had failed. I first attempted to get her to stop criticizing herself so severely. I asked her to write, "I like myself whether I am thin or not." It turned out as I had imagined, she was using her weight as a defense. After writing this affirmation, her responses began to reveal that she could "keep men away" by being fat. When she faced this fact and discussed her fears of men with me, she began to lose some weight. I helped her to speed up the process with the following affirmations:

> *Everything I, Katy, eat turns to health and beauty. My body automatically processes whatever food I eat to maintain my perfect weight which is _____.*

Of course, she also worked on, "I no longer need to fear men."

Katy has now become very interested in caring for her body, which is now twenty pounds lighter, and she has been experiencing a great deal of pleasure in her relationships and sex life.

Obviously sensitivity and a high regard for one's body are very important in achieving sexual satisfaction. This, too, is a part of your self-esteem and sexual identity. A desire to change your body (losing weight, changing your appearance—hair style, using makeup, etc.) is fine as long as you basically accept and appreciate your body first. After all, it is the only body you have right now, so you might as well enjoy it.

Body Image Affirmations

1. I, _____, no longer need to feel anxious about my body.
2. There is nothing at all shameful about my body.
3. I, _____, love all parts of my body.
4. I, _____, like my genitals. (I like my penis / I like my vagina.)
5. I am happy with the size of my breasts (or my penis).
6. My body secretions are acceptable to me.
7. I, _____, value all of my body's tastes and smells.
8. I, _____, realize the natural smell of my genital area is designed to be attractive and it is unnecessary to cover it up.
9. My vagina cleans itself and I do not need douches or deodorants.
10. I, _____, am not embarrassed by my normal menstrual flow.
11. The size of my penis makes no difference to a woman's satisfaction ultimately; or, The size of my

breasts makes no difference to a man's satisfaction ultimately.

12. I, _____, accept nakedness and am no longer inhibited.

13. I, _____, can enjoy being seen in the nude.

14. I, _____, am free and open in regard to my body.

15. I, _____, realize intercourse is not always the ultimate sexual goal for my body.

16. I, _____, know it is more important to feel good about the totality of my own body all the time all day.

17. Since I, have more beauty than ugliness, I will concentrate on my beauty.

18. I, _____, take good care of my body.

Body Sensation

Nancy, age 30, complained of "no feeling" in her vagina. OMG! This might be called "sexual anesthesia." She also said she was aware of constantly holding her vagina very tightly. I began by simply having her write, "I am now beginning to feel sensations in my vagina," to break her of the habit of saying to herself, "I can't feel anything there." What came up to her consciousness from the responses to her affirmations was that her mother had been too terrified to relax and feel anything in her vagina. I felt this was telepathically communicated to her daughter, Nancy. Later in her rebirthing she actually experienced the extreme fear and tightness of her mother's vagina and found it almost impossible to get out of the womb. I developed an affirmation that worked particularly well for her:

> I, Nancy, am not my mother. I can, therefore, relax and let myself feel.

Learning the truth about the situation enabled her to see the inappropriateness of her condition. She stopped mimicking her mother and began to let go. When she communicated everything she had discovered to her husband he was much less critical of her and this, too, helped her a great deal to relax. She reported to me that she was having feeling in her genital area for the first time in her life.

The body is naturally alive with sensitivity. The body can be an ever-increasing source of satisfaction and pleasure. Most of us have never experienced the full potential of sensations available to us. Whether or not you are already experiencing a lot of feeling in your body or whether or not you are suffering from "sexual anesthesia, "these affirmations are for you. No matter how much pleasure you presently allow yourself, you can easily reward yourself with more if you want to.

Body-Sensation Affirmations

1. I, _____, now allow myself to feel much pleasure and sexual energy in my body.
2. Tension no longer robs me of potential pleasure.
3. I, _____, have the natural tendency to feel sexual excitement.
4. I, _____, am becoming more and more aware of the sensations in my genitals.
5. It is okay for me to feel erotically sensitive in other parts of my body than my genitals.
6. My body reacts easily to sexual stimulation. enjoy feeling excitement in every part of my body.
7. My vagina lubricates easily; or, My penis becomes erect when I want it to.
8. My penis stays erect as long as I like; or, My vagina remains moist as long as I like.
9. It is okay for me to feel very aroused.
10. I _____, no longer need to stop the activity that makes me excited.

11. I, _____, am no longer embarrassed by being aroused.

Sex Identity

A 34-year-old woman named Sue complained of having trouble in her relationships with men. She was very bright, well-educated, aggressive, and beautiful—but she felt she "threatened" men, and did not know what to do.

Her sexual history revealed that she strongly over-identified with her father and she seemed to have acquired a great deal of male consciousness, which led her to subtly intimidate men. "Strong in her male side," we would say.

It was difficult to determine this at first because her actions were as feminine as was her shapely body. However, I was able to verify this identification with her father when I did a Rebirthing Session with her. It became very clear that her father had strongly *wanted a boy* and she had picked up on this at the time of birth and had acted it out ever since. Although she had been through many other forms of therapy, she told me this fact had never been so clear to her as it was after her "rebirth."

I was particularly pleased that I had affirmations to give that could help her as she was really afraid she would be over-confronting and competing with men for the rest of her life. Her affirmations were:

I, Sue, no longer have to be a man to please my father.

I, Sue, am developing more girlishness, lady-likeness, and femininity.

I, Sue, no longer need to compete with men.

I, Sue, like being a girl.

After working the affirmations she noticed that she began to stop putting men in the wrong when she was with them. She also stopped indulging herself in criticism of men. Since then she no longer gets comments from men like, "You are too powerful" or "You are too much for me," as she once did, which pleases her very much. She finds that men want to be around her more and writes to me frequently about the good relationship she is now experiencing.

I have observed a great deal of suffering and frustration in many people due to confusion over their sexual identity. A person may be completely unaware of this confusion. For example, as we just saw, a very feminine, beautiful girl may have a great deal of "male consciousness" or vice versa. This is all right unless it acts in any way as an interference in one's relationships with others.

Sex Identity Affirmations

WOMEN

1. It is okay for me to be a woman. woman.
2. I, _____, like being a woman.
3. I, _____, feel strong, and self-assured as a
4. I, _____, like having sex as a woman.

5. It is okay with me to have a woman's body.
6. It is okay with me to have a vagina.
7. It is okay with me to have breasts.
8. I, _____, am not jealous of men for their bodies.
9. I, _____, have control of myself as a woman.
10. I, _____, am a wonderful woman.
11. I, _____, am proud of my sexuality.
12. I, _____, am glad to be alive as a woman.

MEN

1. It is okay for me to be a man.
2. I, _____, like being a man.
3. I, _____, feel strong and self-assured as a man.
4. I, _____, like having sex as a man.
5. It is okay for me to have a man's body.
6. It is okay with me to have a penis.
7. I, _____, am not jealous of the body of a woman.
8. I, _____, have control of myself as a man.
9. I, _____, am a wonderful man.
10. I, _____, am proud of my sexuality.
11. I, _____, am glad to be alive as a man.

Sex Roles

Bridget, age 29, moved to this country from Europe. Her problem was similar to that of several other women I have seen who have been conditioned to believe that women were not supposed to be assertive in sex. Not only that, they were not to have very much fun either. Although Bridget was extremely assertive and independent in all other areas of her life, she was still being passive in sex and not enjoying it. She had orgasms only rarely, after which she experienced some anger at the man, accusing him for somehow making her into something she shouldn't be—a sexy woman in bed. When she wrote affirmations giving herself permission ("It is okay to be assertive, I have the right to initiate sex" etc.) her emotional reactions all centered around being afraid of losing the respect of men if she did this. So then I had her write affirmations such as "I will gain the respect of men if I am seductive and assertive," and the other examples you'll find in this section. Her mind was quite resistant to the affirmations and it was actually a period of months before she tried them out. During that time, however, she did "try out" being more assertive in degrees. Then she suddenly called me in the middle of the night to report that she had just "seduced" a man totally and successfully and she was delighted. He loved it. This breakthrough also helped her to allow herself more fun in bed and once she got out of the sex role stereotype, her orgasms were also easier.

Sex Role Affirmations

1. I, _____, have the right to choose my own role in sex if and when I please.
2. I, _____, have the right to initiate sex and be confident about it without being embarrassed.
3. I, _____, can gain or maintain my partner's respect if I assert myself during sex.
4. Any position in sex is okay and I am free to be dominant or submissive.
5. I, _____, am free to be assertive in sex.
6. As a man, I, _____, am free to be assertive or submissive in my sexuality. I can be submissive and still be masculine when I want to. I can be assertive when I want to.
7. As a woman, I, _____, am free to be submissive or I can be sexually assertive if I want to and still be feminine.
8. Sexual assertiveness is a virtue. I, am now only attracting men who can handle my sexual assertiveness.
9. My sexual appetite is free of my role.
10. My roles in sex are free of the behavior of my parents or friends.
11. I, _____, no longer make my partner into something he or she is not. (I can work out my need for a loving parent at other times.)
12. I, _____, can relax and be myself whenever I want to and my partner has the same right.

Orgasm

Gwendolyn was what some therapists call *primary non-orgasmic;* others would call her *pre-orgasmic.* She called herself "a real failure" as she had never had an orgasm, and none of the previous therapies she had tried had worked for her. She had tried an analyst and a woman's group for pre-orgasmic women, both of which normally produced excellent results. She, however, was in the small minority of 3% failure rate for these groups. This compounded her failure consciousness even more. Her dominant negative thought was, "I can't have an orgasm no matter what."

After I explained to her the principles of metaphysics and how the mind actually rules the body, she agreed to set aside her past failures and listen to me. I reminded her that since she chose to come and see me she must have intuitively known that after all it was possible for her to have an orgasm. I also reminded her that we are by nature orgasmic. The affirmation I gave her was, "I, Gwen, am already orgasmic. All I have to do is go along with it." (Recall the power of the earlier *I am* affirmations.) For Gwen there seemed to be no huge fears or past negative experiences blocking her. Her conviction of "I can't make it," or "I can't do it well enough," was merely a habitual thought pattern. So in her case I gave her just the one affirmation and told her to stick with it. She did. She put it on a recording and used some of her responses as suggestions for alternative affirmations.

One day, not long after, she came into my office with a bottle of champagne. She was as pleased as she was shocked that she had actually had an orgasm despite herself.

The best thing to remember about orgasm is that a great part of it is in the mind and emotions. And then remember that it is okay whichever way you like it. An orgasm is an orgasm is an orgasm. It is interesting to me that so many people are as convinced as ever about women having to have a "penis in the vagina" orgasm even after Masters and Johnson supposedly have convinced the world otherwise. Somehow the message was not made clear enough. Or was it that some people just didn't want to hear it?

In any case, statistics do indicate that the physical source of an orgasm for a woman is based primarily in the clitoris, not in the vagina. Most women like just plain, straight clitoral orgasms. And even later on in the sexual act, a woman's sexual response to having a penis inside her depends very much on how much stimulation her clitoris received before the actual intercourse. Based on the research then, it does seem ridiculous for men to put down women for not experiencing vaginal orgasms and for women to put themselves down for not having them. And yet this still goes on.

However, it is also clear that some women do have and like an orgasm with the penis in the vagina. Either the clitoris was stimulated enough beforehand or the thrusting causes the labia to press against and stimulate the clitoris. (Statistics indicate this is often not as pleasing or intense as direct clitoral orgasm.) Some women are even able to achieve orgasms by stimulation of the breasts alone; some have orgasms in dreams, and others have orgasms without any touching at all from another or themselves. This seems to make it all go back to the mind, right? What is important here is to avoid the temptation of ranking one orgasm as better than another. In actuality, they are all orgasms and it is very destructive to get into any kind of grading system or failure syndrome.

Further, orgasm itself should not be an absolute must. I hate to see people invalidate themselves, totally, just because they are not having orgasms. It would be like hating oneself totally for not playing the piano. So we should not get "fixated" on orgasms. However, they are a natural and highly pleasurable experience and we were born with the natural ability to have them. (Most women have somehow learned how *not* to have them—but we can remedy that!)

But I am really speaking to both sexes about orgasm. Any person suffering with an orgasmic problem really needs to take a look to see what kind of negative payoff he or she may be getting by not having an orgasm. Could it be that you are withholding orgasm to get even in some way? Could it be a form of self-punishment or deprivation? Also, it might be an earlier *personal lie* (a church law, perhaps, that really is a form of *false theology*) that you think you would be breaking, thereby setting up a conflict. Sometimes it is just fear that something terrible will happen physically or emotionally or a fear of losing complete control and/or giving another some power over you. I would like to suggest that everyone take responsibility for his or her own orgasm; leave any blame out of it.

The following affirmations will be very helpful if you use them as I have suggested.

Affirmations About Orgasm

1. It is okay for me to have an orgasm.
2. Orgasm is a feeling of intensely enjoyable pleasure and therefore I do not need to fear it.
3. I, _____, am free to frolic in pleasure.
4. I, _____, do not need to avoid orgasm because of fear any longer; there is nothing to fear.
5. I, _____, now have a clear mental outlook about myself toward orgasms.
6. Having an orgasm is a natural body event; it is a reflex and all I have to do is go along with it.
7. I, _____, am not alarmed if things get blurred as I approach orgasm; this is a sign of coming ecstasy.
8. I, _____, will not experience any disaster if I have an orgasm.
9. I, _____, can have orgasms without any undesirable consequences.
10. It is totally safe to have an orgasm; millions of people have them daily.
11. It is safe to lose temporary control; it helps me to reach ecstasy.
12. Nothing bad will happen if I climax. I have nothing to lose if I climax; I can only win.
13. It is okay if I don't have a coital* orgasm and I am no longer concerned about this.

---

*of or during sexual intercourse

14. I, _____, do not need to hold back and save my orgasms for someone special; I want to experience them now.

15. The more orgasms I experience, the more pleasure I get to enjoy.

16. I, _____, do not need to avoid orgasm because of how I might look, act, or appear; it is okay; my partner likes to see me.

17. I, _____, do not need to withhold orgasm to punish my partner; I can work out my anger at other times and in more appropriate ways.

18. It is not necessary to compulsively strive for simultaneous orgasm with my partner.

19. My life will not change drastically if I have orgasms; it will be just as good; maybe better.

20. I, _____, can take all the time I want in order to have an orgasm.

21. I, _____, like having orgasms.

22. I, _____, can have as many orgasms as I want and I may have orgasms freely any time of the day.

23. I, _____, am okay whether I have an orgasm or not.

24. I, _____, am responsible for my own orgasm, for finding out how I get one, and for communicating to my partner how I get one.

25. The passion of orgasm suspends me from all pain.

26. It is okay for me to be out of control; I am now willing to surrender.

Masturbation

Bob, who was 28-years-old, had masturbated a great deal in his life and had always felt guilty about it. He came to see me because his new girlfriend asked him to show her how he masturbated. He was much too embarrassed to do this in front of her, although the idea of seeing her masturbate excited him. He considered himself liberated and it upset him quite a bit to find that he could not handle her request. After he wrote the affirmation, "It is okay for me to masturbate in front of my partner," he was able to try it once for her. But the experience had brought to his mind many old pictures of himself masturbating in his earlier life, and he had been unable to relax and enjoy himself. He told me about this over the telephone and I suggested that in addition to the first affirmation he also write, "I no longer feel guilty about masturbating in the past." As it turned out, it was unnecessary to see Bob as a client again. He called me back to say that he was now able to masturbate without guilt both privately and in front of his partner and that he was enjoying the new experience immensely, including masturbation during the sexual act.

It is helpful to know that most therapists now are calling masturbation "self-love." However, the old thought patterns often bind us, no matter what new words we use.

Even though masturbation has been and is a world-wide practice, it is still a very sensitive personal subject for most people. By giving yourself love in this way, you are accepting yourself, and accepting responsibility for your needs, your sensuality, your body. Many pre-orgasmic women I have worked with have never tried it, and I must give them "permission" to do so. They are often shocked at the positive and quick results. Many men also feel guilt and shame surrounding the subject which often manifests itself as a hindrance to having sex with others. I hope you will see masturbation as an acceptable avenue to pleasure for yourself and your partner.

Affirmations About Masturbation

1. I, _____, am okay if I masturbate or not.
2. It is perfectly okay to masturbate and explore my body.
3. Since I am truthful about it, there is no need to feel guilty about masturbating as it is a normal part of my own sexual development.
4. Through masturbation I can learn to enjoy my own body; it is fun and pleasurable.
5. Masturbation enables me to learn what techniques are best for arousing my body so that I will be able to show my sexual partner.
6. The more I know my body, the easier it is to show someone else what gives me pleasure.
7. I, _____, allow myself time and space to give
8. pleasure to myself and I feel good about this.
9. Since I am now aware of the truth about it, I,_____, no longer feel guilty about masturbating in the past.

10. It is okay to masturbate in front of my partner.
11. I, _____, deserve pleasure from masturbating.
12. It pleases others for me to please myself.
13. I have the right to enjoy my own genitals.
14. It is natural for me to remember and seek to recreate with my own hand the pleasure I received from my mother's.
15. My mother's hand was innocent, so why should mine be guilty?

Affection

One client could not handle kissing and hugging because his mother always made him hug and kiss his aunts and uncles. Until he got in touch with what was really going on regarding his anger and resentment, his relationships fizzled out continually. He could not understand this for a long time because he knew he was a "good lover."

In this case, it was first necessary for him to handle his anger toward his mother. He needed to do affirmations like "I forgive my mother for making me hug and kiss my aunts when I was little." This brought up a lot of rage for him and it was not until he let it out that he was able to start forgiving her. I encouraged him to continue to let his anger come up and to yell and scream in his car if he needed to. After awhile he was able to sit down with his mother and communicate to her how upset he had been by her demands in this area. This had a very releasing effect upon him. After this he realized that it was inappropriate to withhold affection from the women he cared about just because of those old resentments toward his mother. However, it was a case where he had to almost relearn how to be affectionate. It helped him to write "I now am naturally affectionate in appropriate ways." He came to enjoy it immensely and he began to experience lasting rewarding relationships. His relationship with his mother has also become less strained and much closer.

I am separating affection from foreplay and intercourse because sometimes it helps to find out just exactly where the breakdown lies. I have known men I consider "great" in bed; but who could not handle regular affection on a day-to-day basis. For them it appeared that sex was almost compensatory.

The truth is that most of us are starved for affection. Our parents probably did not feel free to touch us as much as they would have liked because of having to confront incestuous feelings. There is much valid research now about sensory deprivation in infancy. It is no wonder that many of us would actually rather have plain old affection than sex. We want it and yet we often can't handle it because of confusing messages we got when we were little. It is never too late to work this out and you will be very glad you did when you begin to experience the joy in feeling the freedom to touch and hug whomever you like.

Affection Affirmations

1. Physical affection is acceptable in all of my relationships.
2. I, _____, am a good person when I touch myself as well as others.
3. I, _____, am now more and more aware of my need for touching and holding and I am rewarded for expressing that and can communicate that.
4. I, _____, like having a man touch me.
5. I, _____, like having a woman touch me.
6. I, _____, like being held.
7. I, _____, can touch every part of my own body.

8. I, _____, can touch every part of my lover's body.
9. I, _____, am warm.
10. I, _____, am affectionate.

Trust

Mark, age 26, was afraid to let women handle parts of his body. He said he just didn't trust them. His sex history did reveal that his mother never touched his genitals and he felt that had something to do with it. He did not recall any injuries. When I worked with him in the hot tub and he reexperienced his birth, it was very clear that he had been handled much too roughly and that his fear of harm started very early. He also recalled a hernia operation as an infant wherein he developed a fear of nurses who he felt inflicted pain on him in the groin area near the incision. He had then generalized this fear to all women, and even to his girlfriend whom he loved very much. Even she could not be trusted to touch that area. He always experienced terror and would go into a sort of spasm. Writing "I now trust women with my body" was too hard for him so he started out with "I am beginning to trust women with my body." It was also necessary for him to work on these: "I forgive the nurses for hurting me." and "I forgive my mother for avoiding my body when it needed attention." After a while he began to let his girlfriend gently lay her hand on the groin area over the place where he had had an incision. He went through fear at first until I suggested he say the affirmations to himself while she was doing this. He was later able to ask her to gently caress him in that area. This area of his body, so long neglected, needed so much attention that he went through a period of craving to have his genitals held and his groin stroked. He has now gotten over his distrust to the point where he attends sensuous massage courses.

If you find that you trust no one, life will probably be very hard for you. Perhaps you don't trust yourself. If you trust yourself, you will more likely trust others. Things will just work better for you if you have confidence in the natural integrity of another. It is certain that as you like yourself better, you will attract people who are also trustworthy. So don't forget that what you have in front of you is a mirror reflection of "where you are at." In a sexual relationship, people often feel vulnerable and afraid that the other will take advantage of them. This again comes from low self-esteem. So, if you have trouble with these few affirmations, go back and flatten the section on self-esteem again.

Affirmations Regarding Trust

1. I, _____, do trust myself.
2. I, _____, trust myself in bed.
3. I, _____, trust myself in sex.
4. I, _____, trust my partner.
5. I, _____, trust _____ in bed.
6. I, _____, trust _____ in sex.
7. I, _____, trust women.
   I, _____, trust men.
8. My body is safe in the hands of _____.
9. My body is safe in the hands of a man.
   My body is safe in the hands of a woman.

10. I, _____, can trust my partner with my intimate feelings.
11. It is okay to distrust people until they earn my trust.
12. The more I trust people, the more I am rewarded.

Foreplay

I have observed many couples battling over the issue of foreplay. Freda, age 45, and her husband, Stan, were regulars at it. They had done it for years. She complained that he just stuck his penis in without any preparation for her. He complained that he did this because it always took her too long to get stimulated and he gave up long ago trying to get her going. He was convinced that "other women" did not need all of that preliminary stuff even though his experience was limited. She was angry that she was unsatisfied and felt "ripped off." There was little communication between them.

I worked with them separately at first. Stan needed to spend some time learning about the importance of foreplay and he did agree to do some reading from the many good books available. Freda needed to realize that Stan would probably have to experience the joy of foreplay himself before he would be completely aware of its value and be willing to give it. I suggested she take a sensuous massage course and that she start giving more even though she felt she was the one being neglected. I also told her to begin writing "I deserve as much foreplay as I want no matter how long it takes and so does Stan." I asked Stan to write "I can experience pleasure in my own body while I am stroking Freda," and, "It makes me happy to see Freda happy." He also wrote, "Freda deserves the time she needs and so do I." When both of them got out of anger and shifted their positions on the matter even a little, the communication began. Stan also signed up for the massage course.

It must be remembered that the real source of pleasure is in the mind. I am discussing foreplay as a separate issue to think about because so many people I meet are dissatisfied with the amount of time spent in love play. A woman will usually call a man a "good lover" if he spends a lot of time in foreplay, and especially if he enjoys that time spent. If she senses that the man resents it or is doing it only as a favor, she tends to get very upset with him. When both parties are clear about the importance of the clitoris to the woman, there does not seem to be much complaining. A man deserves just as much pleasure in foreplay as a woman. What really matters is how the couple works this out. The "timing" of inserting the penis should be agreeable to both. This is often, however, a source of furious arguments because partners do not communicate their needs and negotiate. (See the section on communication.)

Affirmations About Foreplay

1. I, _____, frequently engage in satisfying and imaginative love play.
2. I, _____, welcome generous, gentle, and effective foreplay.
3. I, _____, deserve all the foreplay I can get and so does my partner.
4. Foreplay is actually love play and my partner and

I mutually enjoy it with or without coitus and orgasm.

5. I, _____, now make sure I get stimulated adequately in foreplay.

6. I, _____ , also make sure my partner gets stimulated enough.

7. I, _____, no longer concern myself with the amount of time it takes to get myself or my partner stimulated.

8. I, _____, always have enough time for sex.

Intercourse

Betty, age 54, came in about six months after separating from her husband of 30 years. Her husband was her first lover and the only one during her marriage. She had been orgasmic a few times during her marriage; however, as she told it, every time she really let go and had fun, her husband would criticize her afterward. He accused her of acting like a prostitute during these times and he would then withdraw. Her conclusion soon was something like this: "When I get really excited, men withdraw their love. Therefore, there must be something wrong with intercourse." However, after many years she decided there was something wrong with her husband and ended the marriage. Shortly after that she had a passionate affair wherein she really let herself go and made love all day, allowing herself abundant orgasms. The next day, however, the man was "unavailable" and could not be reached. He never called her again and this totally reinforced her belief that it was bad to enjoy sex that much and if she did, men would withdraw. When she came to me she was in a sexual relationship with a man she loved; however, whenever she began to let go and approach orgasm, she experienced a big block. After helping her to see how she created the second incident in order to prove herself "right," I gave her the following affirmations which broke the pattern.

1. The more turned on I get the more men like it and want to stay with me.
2. The more I let go, have fun and have orgasms, the more secure my relationship is.
3. I have the right to enjoy intercourse abundantly without any undesirable consequences.

Actually, sex should not be an act, it should be an experience. In other words, it is what it means to you that counts. You could obviously go through all the motions and not have any feelings at all, making it totally mechanical. You can be having heterosexual intercourse and be thinking homosexual thoughts or vice versa. You can—and do have the freedom to—botch it up anyway you want to. Just remember that you are the one who is interpreting it that way. In effect, you are the artist of your own creation.

What can give intercourse a lot of meaning is simply having a full feeling of the total situation here and now. The clearer your mind, the more magical the experience will be. For further understanding, work with the section regarding blocks to experiencing intercourse fully. Since a good part of this book is concerned with sex, it seems unnecessary to write many affirmations here. The list is provided only as a check for yourself to see where you are.

Affirmations On Intercourse

1. I, _____, like making love.
2. I, _____, like intercourse.

3. I, _____, like fucking.
4. I, _____, have the natural tendency to enjoy sex with someone.
5. Sex is natural and spontaneous and I look forward to it.
6. I, _____, have the right to enjoy intercourse abundantly.
7. The more sex I allow myself, the more I can love and be loved.
8. I, _____, am now in touch with everything that is going on when I make love. My mind is not somewhere else, it is on my present experience.
9. I, _____, feel it rather than think about it.
10. Oral stimulation can be very effective and I am de-
11. lighted about it.
12. I, _____, have no resistance to trying oral and anal sex. And I reserve the right to say no to it if I do not like it.

Negative Past Experiences

Mary, a 31-year-old divorcee, complained of having a lot of fear whenever she made love. She was only able to pinpoint it as far as saying that she "feared something terrible would happen" afterward. She did not recall having been caught or punished for sexual play as a child, nor did she have an idea what the terrible thing might be.

In order to quickly find out what was behind this fear, I asked her to begin writing right away: "I, Mary, no longer need to fear anything when I make love." Her responses came up revealing a fear of being punished, especially beaten. She then did recall that her father punished her by beating her and that he often came into her bedroom to do it. The fact that she was sometimes beaten for things she considered pleasurable led her to conclude that pleasure led to punishment, especially if there were any connection to bedrooms. I suggested that for one thing she begin to have sex outside of her bedroom. She noticed a marked improvement, less fear. She then worked on the following affirmations:

> ❖ *My bedroom is a safe and pleasurable place to be.*

- *My bedroom is no longer a place of punishment. It is a place of reward.*
- *I now forgive my father for beating me.*
- *Other men are not my father and I do not need to fear them.*

For the first time in her life she began to spend some time relaxing in her bedroom. She redecorated it in a sensual, cheerful manner and put fresh flowers by her bed. She had long relaxing talks with her friends there and eventually entirely let go of the fear which had loomed over her.

Our past is always with us even though we modify it with what happens in the present. As we have mentioned, old thought patterns can continue to produce results even though we are no longer thinking them. By the same token, we can still be acting out old relationships even though these people are not present. These things are revealed to me over and over again when I take a client's sexual history. When I ask that person to describe his or her first childhood sex experience, I see that the conclusions made right after that experience are often still producing results years and years later. And yet, you do not have to stay stuck in the past. If you change the generalizations now that you made in the past you can, in effect, change the past. Since we carry our consciousness with us wherever we go and produce the same results over and over, it is obvious that it is only when we change our consciousness that we can expect permanent replacements of old negative patterns. This is why affirmations are so powerful.

Affirmations Regarding Negative Past Experiences

1. I, _____, forgive myself for (fill in a particular negative past experience).
2. I, _____, am now free of the past regarding my emotionally negative sexual experiences. I always focus on the value I learned from them.
3. I, _____, no longer focus on the losses I have suffered in the past. Instead, I hold on to those things that are of value to me.
4. My early painful sexual experiences do not make me a failure in sex.
5. Since I am responsible for my action, I, _____, don't need to be guilty about anything.
6. I, _____, now forgive men for their ignorant behavior toward me. I, _____, am no longer angry at men; I feel loving toward them. I feel do not need to get even with men any longer; I can let them love me.
7. I, _____, now forgive women for their ignorant behavior toward me. I, _____, feel loving toward them. I, _____, am no longer angry at women. I do not need to get even with women any longer. I can let them love me.
8. My bedroom and bed is a safe and pleasurable place to be.
9. My bedroom is no longer a place of punishment, deprivation or restriction. It is a reward, a place for rest, relaxation, pleasure and inspiration.
10. I have the right to enjoy my bed and bedroom alone in privacy or with anyone I choose and for any purpose or enjoyment.
11. I no longer transfer my strong negative feelings about elimination and body secretions to my sexual

functioning. I feel okay about these things. My organs and their functions are fine with me.

12. My body is mine to use and enjoy as I please. What my parents have said is not what makes me decide whether or not to have intercourse. I am free to revoke and reverse any earlier beliefs.

13. It is no longer appropriate for me to feel resentment toward my parents nor my lover while I am in bed. I now feel warmth, harmony, kindness, and love.

14. I, _____, now forgive my parents for using withdrawal of love as a way of disciplining me.

15. I, _____, now forgive my parents for their ignorant behavior toward me.

16. I, _____, now forgive my parents and others for teaching me negative things about sex.

17. I, _____, am now receiving so much success and satisfaction that I don't care if I get even or not.

18. I, _____, no longer use what happened to me in the past as a cop out.

19. I, _____, now fully forgive myself for not enjoying myself and my body the way I really wanted to.

Fears

Janet, age 26, was a beautiful young woman who had been a model. She had no trouble attracting men, yet she was very afraid to let go and have an orgasm. In talking with her, she did not seem to have the common fears of getting hurt, getting pregnant, getting dependent, or the like. She told me that all she could say was that as she got close to orgasm, she experienced fear and she could not understand what it was related to. I asked her to write the simple affirmation: "I, Janet, no longer fear letting go and having an orgasm." After writing this about fifteen times, the truth came to the surface in her responses. What she was afraid of was appearing "ugly" in front of a man. She thought that the facial grimaces she had seen in pictures of people as they experienced orgasm were ugly and she was afraid to look different from her perfectly made up mirror image. Her fear of becoming ugly encompassed all areas of her life. It was obvious to me that she needed to raise her self-esteem without being purely dependent on her beauty.

When I assured her that men did not find the facial expression of sexual pleasure ugly—that it was quite the opposite—she would not believe me. She was afraid to take a chance. Nevertheless, she did want to have orgasms, so she tried writing the affirmations anyway, to see if that fear really was the problem. She wrote:

- ❖ I, Janet, no longer fear losing _____'s approval.
- ❖ The more I let go, the more beautiful men find me.
- ❖ My worth as a woman does not depend on my physical beauty.
- ❖ Having orgasms increases my beauty.
- ❖ I no longer fear being impotent.

Janet was not only able to finally have orgasms, she also gave up some of her superficial "act" and enjoyed life more.

- ❖ I, _____, know that I am naturally potent as soon as I let myself be.
- ❖ I, _____, no longer fear being sexually inadequate. I just let go and relax.
- ❖ I, _____, no longer fear being frigid. I really am more erotic than I can imagine.

Look into your life and see how often you have thoughts of fear. Fear can be a very destructive force. Fear is the absence of self-love, self-approval, and self- esteem. Fear in the mind disturbs the entire makeup of your being. If you want greater health, happiness, peace of mind and wonderful sex, liberate yourself from your ungrounded fears. You can do this by facing them and replacing them with new thoughts of confidence and safety. I have placed in this chapter affirmations to dispel some common fears people repeatedly have pertaining to sex. There are many others dispersed throughout the other sections of the book and you can add more anti-fear affirmations of your own. Although it is true that fear can serve you by putting you on guard of impending danger, to allow it to absorb and hinder your natural desires and functions will keep you forever in bondage. Fear without cause can be your greatest enemy.

Affirmations Regarding Fears

1. My sexuality no longer scares me. I, no longer run from it. (Instead I welcome and look forward to experiencing it.)
2. I, _____, no longer fear being sexually inadequate. I just let go and relax.
3. I, _____, no longer fear being frigid. I really am more erotic than I can imagine.
4. I, _____, no longer fear being impotent. I know that I am naturally potent as soon as I let myself be.
5. Intercourse no longer frightens me. I, can have it and be positively rewarded for it.
6. I, _____, no longer fear orgasm. It is fun and pleasurable.
7. The sex act no longer produces concern about loss and/or death. It is an act of aliveness and physical honor.
8. I, _____, no longer fear losing _____, or his approval. I now am fully approved of by him and by me.

   I, _____, no longer fear losing _____, or her approval. I am now fully approved of by her and me.

9. I, _____, no longer fear being rejected when I express my sexual desires and preferences.

10. My sex partners love and accept me more for expressing my sexual desires, fantasies, and preferences.

11. I, _____, no longer fear women, envy, or hate them. or

    I, _____, no longer fear men, envy, or hate them.

12. I, _____, now feel safe around men/ women because I enjoy myself and I enjoy them.

13. I, _____, no longer fear appearing stupid or silly in front of _____.

14. I, _____, am now very poised, charming, and relaxed in front of those to whom I am most attracted—especially during intercourse.

15. I, _____, am no longer threatened by (See what fear comes out here.)

16. I, _____, no longer fear losing control to _____. I have control of myself.

17. I, _____, am always in self-control.

18. I, _____, no longer fear anything about sex. That is inappropriate.

19. Sexual intercourse is an appropriate form of adult behavior and pleasure, especially for me.

20. I, _____, no longer have to fear pregnancy when I make love; I am responsible about birth control and always enjoy having my monthly period. or

    I, _____, no longer have to fear getting a girl pregnant when I make love; I am responsible about birth control.

21. I, _____, am no longer afraid of being punished for sex; I look forward to being rewarded.
22. I, _____, am no longer frightened about exploring something new in sex; I am willing to experiment.
23. I, _____, now can replace all my fears with love and self-esteem.

Potency

Dick is a 33-year-old psychologist with a long history of premature ejaculation. I found him to be extremely bright, personable, and aware. Because of his background, he had an extra amount of insight into himself. He had also taken part in several therapies including having gone with his wife to Masters and Johnson in Missouri for treatments. While he was there he did have some relief from premature ejaculation; however upon returning home the problem recurred. It became quite obvious to both of us as we talked that his problem had to do with the fact that his mother had threatened him regarding intercourse as a teenager. She would say "If you get a woman pregnant, I'll kill you!" The fear he felt had been so strong that even though he knew that the threat was no longer real and that the fear was no longer appropriate, he was unable to get out of the pattern. I asked him to write these affirmations:

> ❖ *I, Dick, can ejaculate in a woman's vagina without any undesirable consequences.*
> ❖ *I, Dick, no longer have to worry about getting a woman pregnant. (His wife was on adequate birth control.)*

❖ I, Dick, am no longer affected by my mother's threats.

❖ I, Dick, am in control of my own genitals.

After a short talk with his wife I sensed it was also necessary for her to work on the following affirmation, "I am willing for Dick to get over this." She was amazed at what I had perceived and did confess to me that she was, in fact, afraid that if he did get over his problem that he might begin sleeping around with other women.

I recently received a letter from them saying that the problem now seemed to be permanently resolved.

Men often think that their impotency problems are the cause of all the feelings of failure they have and of all the emotional pain they experience. Actually, the reverse is probably true; the problem usually stems from, or is caused by, feelings of failure-and emotional pain they already had prior to the first experience of impotency. It can also be due to old irrational fears that no longer apply. If a man had a great fear of displeasing his mother about anything when he was young, for example, he might be tense in the presence of all women and unable to be natural. Or the problem might also be due to an unwillingness to give the woman pleasure because she somehow reminds him too much of his mother. He may still want to "get even" with his mother or he may even have suppressed incestuous feelings toward her.

This particular subject is one that most people do not feel comfortable discussing, even if they have not experienced it. The very word "impotent" is enough to panic many men. However, I have seen amazing ill results in this area when men have first worked with the self-esteem affirmations in the first section and then go on to some more specific ones like these that follow. If you are impotent, you may tend to think it pointless writing the affirmation "I am potent." Do it anyway. Remembering past experiences of impotency or thinking of yourself as permanently impotent will keep you in a downward spiral. Think potent; your body will always obey your mind.

Affirmations Regarding Potency

1. I, _____, no longer fear being impotent. I am master of my own body.
2. I, _____, am now satisfied that I am potent because I am master of my own body and its functions.
3. I, _____, have control over my own genitals.
4. I, _____, can become erect when I want to and stay erect as long as I like.
5. I, _____, can let go and climax when I choose. (The more I relax, the easier it is.)
6. I, _____, am highly pleasing to myself in the presence of women.
7. My potency has nothing to do with my financial status, my social status, or religious status.
8. My partner enjoys my orgasms.
9. It is okay to have intercourse with the woman I love.
10. I, _____, no longer unconsciously punish my mate. I reward her by achieving an erection.
11. I, _____, no longer need to display my anger when in bed. I can work out my suppressed hostility at other times and in more appropriate ways.
12. I, _____, no longer fear being dominated by women or men.

13. Having an orgasm will not rob me of any energy I need in order to do other things. The opposite is true—orgasms are energizing.
14. I, am now developing a success consciousness about sex.
15. I, _____, am potent and powerful.
16. My mind rules my body when I want it to.

Suppressed Incest

Jerome, age 28, claimed his relationships with women were unsuccessful. He noted, while doing his sexual history, that most of the women he was attracted to were like his sister or at least, somehow, reminded him of her. He recalled always feeling very attracted to his sister, however, he had never "done anything" with her. In fact, they had never seen each other in the nude as nudity was totally forbidden in his family.

When I encouraged him to talk about his incestuous feelings toward his sister, he was very reluctant. After he wrote, "I am now willing to experience my incestuous feelings toward my sister," things were different and he came back to me relating many old fantasies and several recent dreams. I encouraged him to continue letting these feelings come up, and giving himself permission via affirmations. One day he suddenly made the decision to fly home and visit his sister. He sat down with her and confessed to her all his past incestuous feelings, feeling much relieved at having done so. Right before he left he took off all his clothes and stood in front of her in the nude, acting out some. thing he had long ago wanted to do. The next day after leaving, however, he broke out in a rash all over and later learned that she did the same. He admitted to me that he probably had overdone it. Anyway, he said he felt like a new person for finally confessing his feelings. Letting go of all that guilt freed him to the point that he shortly thereafter attracted a new girlfriend with whom he is having a totally satisfying relationship.

Suppressed incest always stands in the way of sexual affection.

Do you deny having these suppressed feelings? Consider this: If you relax and let anyone rub your body long enough, you will get sexual feelings—even from a dog's warm body! So why shouldn't the warm bodies of your parents have stimulated sexual feelings? The subconscious does not distinguish whether the "warm body" was your parent or not. In the same way any affection or love has the natural tendency to bring up sexual feelings. It is just normal to feel attracted whether it is the same sex or not.

If you deny yourself sex fantasies regarding your parents or children, then every time you touch them your feelings will be inhibited and natural human warmth is being blocked. Obviously, it is possible to have natural human warmth toward them without sexual fantasies. However, if you stop suppressing sexual feelings as you probably have been, there will be more naturalness. It certainly does not mean that you have to act out these fantasies just because it would be pleasurable. You can resolve these feelings by just letting them surface. And if you have no blocks in touching your parents or children, then there will be almost no blocks in touching your lover. On the other hand, if you have inhibited these feelings and kept them unresolved, you will experience discomfort touching your parents or children because the fear of having to confront these feelings will manifest itself in you. What is likely to happen then, is that this fear becomes generalized toward everybody. How often do we feel that we can naturally touch anyone? (I recommend you do these affirmations even if your parents are no longer alive.)

Affirmations to Clear Suppressed Incest

1. I, _____, can have sexual feelings toward my parents without acting them out.
2. It is also okay for me to act out my sex fantasies about my parents with my lover instead.
3. If I, _____, have committed acts of incest, it is okay to forgive myself even if I enjoyed it and/or whether I initiated it or not.
4. Just because I've committed acts of incest in the past, does not mean that I will do it again.
5. It is okay to have sexual fantasies about my father. It is okay to have sexual fantasies about my mother. Just because it is okay does not mean I actually have to act them out.
6. I, _____, am now willing to experience my incestuous feelings about my mother, father, brothers and sisters, children, etc.

Verbal Communication About Sex

Jill is a common example of someone who comes in complaining that she is not getting what she wants from sex with her husband. I inquired if she had ever asked for what she wants. Her reply was "Oh, I couldn't do that. It would hurt his feelings if he knew I don't like it the way he is doing it." I reminded her that if she keeps on pretending it is okay, her partner is likely to keep on doing what he is doing since he thinks she is pleased. She kept protesting that he was "too sensitive." When she wrote, "I am free to discuss all aspects of sex with my partner," she saw from her own responses that it had nothing at all to do with the fragility of her partner. She saw that the problem was her own embarrassment. She just was not comfortable talking about sex at all. I encouraged her to write the affirmations which follow and put them on tape.

She began to discuss sex with her friends and was amazed to find out how much they, too, wanted to talk about the subject. She began to take responsibility and to stop blaming her partner. She joined a women's group and gained further courage. She finally wrote her desires down on a list and asked her husband to do the same, after which they swapped lists. This made it easier for her to open communication. He was, in fact, very relieved to know what her true desires were and was eager to fulfill them.

It is very important for you to develop the freedom to discuss all aspects of sex with your partner. I know how hard this is since every client I have ever had, without exception, found this to be very difficult. Even ten sex therapists themselves listed verbal communication as one thing they would most like to improve on in their own sex lives. Once you get over your initial fears of embarrassment or hurting the other, you will find it much easier than you had thought. Don't pass over these affirmations lightly. You would be cheating yourself. There is something very magical about open communication regarding sex. You will reap benefits beyond your imagination.

Affirmations on Verbal Communication About Sex

1. I, _____, have a natural tendency to be open and honest in my communication regarding sex.

2. I, _____, feel free to discuss all aspects of my sex life with my partner.

3. I, _____, can now easily expose my feelings and fears.

4. I, _____, am now learning to express my own sexual needs and desires as valid.

5. I, _____, am no longer afraid to ask for what feels good. I can easily tell my partner what feels good and communicate my sexual wishes easily.

6. It is okay to communicate my sexual needs to _____. It is not selfish of me to say "I want."

7. Whenever I, _____, hesitate in the verbalization of my sexual feelings, I will agree to probe deeper.

8. I, _____, no longer feel uncomfortable when asking for information about sex.

9. I, _____, am able to put my feelings into words.

10. I, _____, have the right to say *no* without losing my partner's love.

11. I, _____, acknowledge my partner verbally whenever I like what is being done.

12. I, _____, am secure enough to admit it when I feel vulnerable and need love.

13. I, _____, get rewarded for revealing my feelings.

14. I, _____, no longer blame. I look at what thoughts are going on with me.

15. I, _____, have a right to express my true feelings wherever I am, no matter whom I am with.

Interferences and What Do About Them

As I work with people, I tend to see over and over again some common blocks to sexual fulfillment. I call these the "eight biggies." Actually one could list hundreds of blocks; I am sure you have found your own after working with this book. But I would like to make sure that you are clear on these most common blocks before closing. I will list them first before giving the appropriate affirmations.

1. Thinking during sex rather than feeling.

It is just amazing what people have on their minds during sex. Often it has nothing to do with sex at all. Or if it does, the thoughts are often negative— "I can't," "What if I don't?" "I wonder if I am doing it right!" "What will he think if _____?" "What does she think of me now?" "Am I pleasing him?" and on and on and on. All of these kinds of things are distractions and are negative suggestions on one's consciousness. They will produce failures and difficulties.

2. Worrying about time during sex.

Somehow we have the notion that if it takes five more minutes to have an orgasm our partner will be bored. What is five minutes out of twenty-four hours anyway? Think of the small amount of time you spend having sex (which is fun and free) in relation to other things you spend time on. Squeezing it in somewhere is not very ideal. Not staying in the present time is the other damaging thing here. What works is focusing on this *very second.*

3. Stopping that which is making you very excited and doing something else.

For example, if a man is stimulating his partner just right, on the clitoris, and she is getting very excited, he often will get excited, too, and stop to insert his penis. This interruption will often ruin things for her. The moral is that when you feel very excited continue doing what you are doing. An orgasm will surely follow.

4. Not taking turns.

When both are trying to do everything at once, it is very confusing. It is hard to be a giver and a receiver at the same time. What I suggest is that one person gives first and the other receives with pleasure. And then they switch. What works best is two people (two minds) concentrating on one body at once. When you are the receiver, you concentrate on yourself. Your "giver" will be also concentrating on you and this is very powerful in energy flow.

5. Not getting heavy feelings out of the way before starting sex.

Very often the whole thing just never gets off the ground because there is such a barrier of unexpressed feelings between the partners. Even if what needs to be expressed may not pertain to the other at all, it still needs to be expressed. Whatever it is that prevents either of you from being "here now" should be aired first—even if it is frustration about work or whatever. And for sure, angry, hurtful, or frightening feelings can be let in. In this light you will note that often after intense sharing, you will feel very turned on.

6. Not asking for what you want.

People often expect their partners to be omnipotent and just imagine that he or she will somehow automatically know what is most pleasurable for them. Then if it does not turn out, they might even decide that that person just was not a good lover. It is so simple to state one's preference in the beginning of a new relationship. For example "What really turns me on is _____,"does not hurt the other's ego and, in fact, the other is usually delighted to know. Even in more established relationships, preferences change and this should be communicated continually.

7. Not making agreements.

When certain agreements are made it is a great relief not to have to worry about them during the sex act. For example, if a woman is constantly worried that it is taking her too long to have an orgasm, this will certainly detract from her experience. A simple agreement such as each giving the other the right to stop if he or she is tired is good. That way, the woman in the case above would have certainty that as long as her mate was still participating, she does not have to worry about his being tired. If he ever did stop (which probably would be not very often) she could finish by masturbating, as long as they also had that agreement. Another excellent agreement is that each would only do what they liked to do. This avoids interfering thoughts such as "I wonder if he is bored," or "I wonder if he likes that really, maybe he is just trying to please me."

8. Not being clear on each other's purpose for sex.

If one person has it that sex is strictly for pleasure and the other still has the dominating thought that it is ultimately for procreation and the rest is only a favor, you can see where resentments would be easily built up. Or one may be using sex as a way to get love and the other as a way to dominate. Here again, the wires are crossed and the flow of energy lessened. It would be a good idea for both to sit down and clear this. (Better late than never.) One fun thing to do is to take out a piece of paper and write down the following: "My purposes for having sex are:" and just begin listing whatever comes to mind. Then each discusses what is on his or her paper or they simply exchange papers.

Here are some appropriate affirmations:

1. I,_____, am now always concentrating on my sensations, not my thoughts when I make love.
2. I, _____, no longer exert conscious intellectual control over the sexual experience. I just feel.

3. I, _____, now put my total attention on the area of the body that is being stimulated.

4. I, _____, no longer am a "spectator," "judge," and "jury" of my sexual performance or my partner's. I just relax and feel it.

5. I, _____, am no longer afraid of asking for too much nor taking too much time. I deserve all I can get.

6. I, _____, avoid creating pressure and tension prior to the act of lovemaking.

7. I, _____, do not allow my mate to pressure me. I am free to explore my own way in sex without being pressured.

8. I, _____, avoid creating pressure and tension prior to the act of lovemaking. I now always create a relaxed mood.

9. I, _____, no longer stop or change the activity that makes me excited; I communicate to my partner that I want to continue.

10. When I am very excited, I keep right on doing what I am doing some more. When my partner gets very excited the same is true.

11. When it is my turn to receive, it is perfectly okay to concentrate totally on myself.

12. I, _____, don't have to please my partner the same moment he or she is pleasing me. I can relax and enjoy myself and please him or her later.

13. I, _____, am more and more aware of my feelings before having sex and am willing to express them if I know they are going to interfere.

14. I, _____, have the right to clear my head before beginning sex and so does my partner. It is okay to take time for this.

15. The more I share verbally, the better sex I will have.
16. It is okay to make love whether I am psychologically disturbed or not.
17. I, _____, now take the responsibility to communicate my wishes and desires in sex. I have a right to ask for what I want.
18. I, _____, now take responsibility to make any agreements that will ease my mind and help me to relax more.
19. Whenever I get worried or concerned about something in sex, I communicate it and make an agreement with my partner as to how to solve it so that both of us win.
20. My purpose for sex is to have fun and increase our Joy.

Final Affirmations

I am the artist of my own creation.

I now take the responsibility for my own fulfillment in love, and for my own sexual well-being and pleasure.

I deserve love.

I deserve sexual pleasure.

Part Four

The Rainbow Millennium

Sexual Preferences

No book on Love and the fulfillment of your sex-life in this millennium would be complete without mentioning the wide range of sexual preferences that are available to you in the 21st century. As I was a pioneer back in the 1970's being honest about such things as sexual pleasure, fantasies, masturbation, sexual intercourse, affection, and how our thoughts create the reality for us in these areas, I would be amiss in 2019 not to mention the wide variety of sexual preferences and choices available in this internet and smart-phone age. Although Markus and I have chosen a Sacred, Heterosexual Monogamy as our preference, we are not opposed nor critical of other preferences that people have taken over the past 40 years since I first published I Deserve Love. There is a wide range of choices that still demand we Love ourselves and the choices we have made—simultaneously.

Nowadays, most of us heterosexuals have the inner peace of accepting that the LGBTQ community is legitimately deserving of our blessings. Back in the 1970's, homosexuality was still viewed by many as "deviant behavior," and in some cases even treated as an illness. Those days are gone in the USA, and we set the standard for the rest of the world in this broad based tolerance of people's various life choices and identities, most of all in their sexual preferences and inclinations.

The choices are many. But basically we embrace the freedom of choice, or the freedom of being as you like, without harm to others in this choice. We did a Sex and Money Seminar in Copenhagen a few years ago, and this opened up a whole can of sexual preferences we could not embrace. One of the men in the training was involved in a sadomasochism ring, and enjoyed inflicting pain on women. This preference we do not embrace. In no way shape or form do we support inflicting pain on others, even if they are "asking for it," and calling that Love. In this we draw the line. Love is pain free, in our book. Sex that leads to mutual Joy and feeling Well and Good in our body is pleasurable and Loving. Actions that place one partner dominating over another, and furthermore deriving "pleasure from pain" is upside down thinking and feeling in our opinion. This book is not promoting these kinds of sexual preferences.

Lesbian, Gay, Bisexual, Transgender, and "Questioning" or Queer—LGBTQ—is the new standard of acceptance. Monogamous marriage is often desired and practiced in these areas of preference. Even parenting and adoption. These are some of the colors of the Rainbow Millennium. But the colors do not stop there. Some are exploring the parameters of polyamorous relationships with multiple partners. Apps like Tinder and Bumble and Plenty of Fish are just a few of the platforms people are using to hookup. Although we are not using these in our own life, there are many options out there to explore.

What we have found in our work is that people want a deep connection. They want good communication, and they want an intimacy that transcends mere sex and physical affection—they want spiritual intimacy that gives their soul a sense of peace and fulfillment. We wrote a whole book called Spiritual Intimacy: What You Really Want With A Mate. When we teach A Course in Miracles principles in the LRT®, we discuss the ego's mindset or thought system versus the Holy Spirit's thought system. The ego leads to struggle, suffering, sorrow and eventually death. The Holy Spirit leads to deep ease, feeling good, perfect health, more joy, and immortal life. The only thing we say in the LRT about sex is, "Are you in the ego's thought system around it or the Holy Spirit's thought system?" Only you can decide that, whether you are Gay, Straight, Polyamorous, or otherwise. Your preference does not matter as much as the purpose and premise on which you base your sex-life. Is it based on unconditional Love, or is it still racked with the uncertainties, fears, unfulfillments and false motives of the ego?

One client of ours in Australia came for a session. When we interviewed her on her profession, she informed us she was a single mom, and was working as a high end call girl. She had absolutely no shame or guilt about this career choice. She had no shame or guilt about sex, that we could tell, nor was she looking to do something else for her job that was more honorable. Prostitution was not a dirty word in her book. She was good at her craft and it paid very well.

Noticing she was attractive and with a voluptuous figure, we asked her if any of her clients fell in love with her and wanted more than just sex. She said, "Yes, and that can be a problem. But I don't let it get in the way of my work." In the end, though, she was still looking for a relationship, and this was the main thing she came to us for help. Her problem was not sexual, but more trusting that an emotional relationship would not make her dependent on a guy and leave her with no financial freedom. In this case her choice of lifestyle and mode of earning her living was kind of a catch 22. It gave her financial freedom, but it kept away the one with whom she could have a lasting relationship. Therefore, she had remained single for a long time. Would there be a man who accepted her profession? Now that is a preference that would be very different than the norm. Perhaps there would be a man out there willing to share her, but probably not. We asked for a miracle.

Another client of ours showed up at a long term training we were holding in Glastonbury, England. In one of the first Rebirthing Exchanges I went into his room and asked him, "What's coming up for you?" His Rebirther, who was new in her practice, needed support. He confessed he "had been a girl, but now he is a boy." WOW, this was the first transgender case I had so close to me. I took a breath and supported him in accepting his new gender. I also encouraged him to start a Rebirthing practice to help other transgender people come to grips with their decision to cross over. Healthy sexuality in his case was dependent on him making this shift at the body level to change genders and be the sex that he felt comfortable in, not the one he was born in. This was a new one for me, but I handled it. Now he is developing a Breathwork practice and helping those like himself with Self-Love and acceptance.

The point I am making here is that there are a lot of sexual preferences out there now that were traditionally frowned upon, or deemed immoral, or screwed up, and now they are entering into more of a middle zone of acceptance. *I Deserve Love* applies to everyone. The one thing that defines Love is a state of Joy, free of pain, and in the vibration of giving and receiving. So if your sexual preference falls within that broad range of qualities, you deserve Love in the manner that you define it and desire it.

Affirmations on Sexual Preference

1. I, _____, am innocent for being gay.
2. I, _____, am innocent for being lesbian.
3. I, _____, make my sexual preference in joy and harmony.
4. Giving love and receiving love are one in me.
5. Now that I accept and embrace my sexuality, I can express it however I want to.
6. My sexuality brings Joy to my mate, and heals both of us of all pain.
7. Now I am the gender I was always meant to be.
8. I can be giving sexual pleasure to others and maintain my center and innocence.
9. I deserve to be well provided for in life, no matter what my sexual preference is.
10. Using my sexuality to earn money is innocent; I consider it a sacred art.
11. I, _____, now embrace my sexual preference fully and with power.
12. I, _____, am always innocent using sex to express my joy.

Great Sex Over Sixty

Although I never give my age being an Immortalist (in the vibe of the ageless), I openly admit I found Markus "late in life." I was "in my sixties," you might say. And furthermore, he was in his fifties, so there was more than a decade between our ages. But that did not matter in the least bit. We knew we had a Divine Purpose for being together, and this brought us immense joy and satisfaction. We knew our Spiritual Masters put us together, so you might say we had an arranged marriage. It was awesome then, and still is. We got married officially in Herakhan, Babaji's ashram, on April 4th, 2009, after being together more than a year. And this year, 2019, we are coming up on our 10th year wedding anniversary. In India as well. Awesome again!

When Markus came to me from Philadelphia, I was living in Marina Del Rey in Los Angeles. He had been studying with his Spiritual Master, Tara Singh, for 17 years. He also was completing a thirty-year marriage that was his "old life." He brought with him very little baggage—literally and figuratively speaking. He arrived with two suitcases, a few choice books, two leather jackets (one brown and one black), and a set of Henkel kitchen knives. I thought that was funny at the time, but we actually needed the knives. He left everything else, including two properties, and two vehicles, to his X wife. We felt so free. Unencumbered by anything. It was wonderful. We would take long walks together and go out on the Marina Del Rey pier, inhaling the ocean air and appreciating the remarkable view—it was so romantic.

Markus, having been with Tara Singh for all those years, who was celibate by the time of his teaching mission, was looking at this issue of sex in our relationship. He said to me, on one of our early morning walks, "I am not too much into celibacy." WOW. Well, when I really looked at the issue myself, I had been single for many years and was focused on my mission. I felt so close to Babaji and the Divine Mother I did not really feel I was "missing out" by not having a sex-life. But now the game had changed! For the first time I was in a Relationship that felt totally aligned with this mission, and how we would define it would be very important. Our relationship would actually be the model for what we were to teach and share with the world. What about sex? We wanted to be conscious about it.

After menopause my sex drive really decreased. I did not feel like I needed it to feel fulfilled. I had other things to do in the mission—getting people to India, to Babaji's feet, spreading the LRT and Rebirthing worldwide, writing books, traveling around the world—I was never bored nor did I ever feel like I was missing out. My life was what is always had been. "More fun per hour." But then Markus came, along with a relationship in the New Paradigm for me—a game changer, to say the least! Immediately our intimacy was in the forefront of my life, and this included sex!! So I just kept surrendering to this new development. And it was fun.

Our intimacy began with the most important factors already in place. 1) We felt a deep connection from the heart. 2) We agreed to have a "conflict-free" relationship. 3) We engaged in great and honest communication about everything, and had the means to process ourselves on our issues through Liberation Breathing and other spiritual practices. 4) We put our Spiritual Mission in the first place, and this invoked in us what we now call "Spiritual Intimacy." And 5) We were very loving and patient with one another to discover the best rhythm and joy for sexual pleasure and expression in our new relationship.

At first we were more into oral sex, as I had a history of cystitis and this would sometime flare up from penetration. But Markus was so sweet and loving on this point. He said, "Let's not make it a problem." And the other thing was for me the environment. It has to be in the right vibe. Sometimes on the road we are not in a hotel or a person's home that is conducive to sexual intimacy. I have to have everything perfect, in a holy way, and feel the surroundings support our love making. (Perhaps that is just overcompensating for my "personal lie," "I'm not perfect.") When I have this right on, I can get in the mood quite easily.

Without getting too explicit about the whole thing, oral sex is fantastic. I love giving and receiving it, and Markus loves giving and receiving it as well. It is great in all kinds of settings, especially at home, where we have "prepared every room for God." In India the Lingam and the Yoni are honored in a sacred way, and in oral sex we just transfer this sacred honoring of the Male and Female principles to our sex-life. We consider all sex acts to be ones of deep and fulfilling Sacred Worship. This is what sex should be, and this is what it was designed to be by our Creator—an instant "nirvana on earth," based on the orgasmic bliss we were given by God to be one of our greatest human Joys.

As I said after menopause my body changed. I did not have the sex-drive so much, and also my vagina would not lubricate like it used to. But again, Markus, said, "Let's not make it a problem." We use a fantastic personal lubricant called Astroglide®. It is water based and not sticky, or thick. It tastes ok and they even have strawberry flavor. It is so slippery I can hardly believe it, and using it makes penetration pleasurable and easy. I was amazed.

The other thing that is important to know, you guys over sixty, there is usually only one speed that works for women in sex at this age, or possibly any age—and this speed is SLOW! Foreplay begins with "taking out the trash," one of my girlfriends once said. So you have to have the whole day in harmony, and by the time you get around to the actual lovemaking, there is clear space and a feeling of relaxation and beauty. Markus has always been sensitive to my rhythms, and accepts my desire for everything to be just right in the timing and the environment.

Foreplay is essential. Building up to penetration is a must. This is why we like oral sex so much. It opens everything up. And then penetration is naturally flowing, and even that has to be slow, in degrees. Play some great music as well. We love Classical Indian Music during love-making. It starts out so slow, and builds in rhythm and intensity, just like the act of lovemaking itself. Light a few candles. Make sure the room is neat, and all other things put away. In order to have great sex you have to have a great environment and atmosphere. What would be a great atmosphere for you? It has to suit both of you. If one partner likes to play "rock and roll" and the other likes "classical," you might have to work out a deal and play "easy jazz." This whole thing is a beautiful dance then, and the results will be that your sex life takes you to the stars.

Affirmations on Great Sex Over Sixty

1. I, _____, have great sex at my age.
2. I, _____, never let my age stop me from enjoying sex.
3. I, _____, deserve to have a great sex-life over sixty.
4. My sex life is better now that I have more wisdom.
5. I, _____, give my partner what he/she wants.
6. I, _____, always ask for what I want in sex.
7. Sex rejuvenates my mind and body.
8. Sex keep me young; I youth while having sex.
9. I, _____, see our lovemaking as a form of Divine Worship.
10. I, _____, am relaxed in sex, which makes me even more relaxed in life.
11. Sex is sacred, therefore I treat all things around our lovemaking in a sacred manner.
12. I, _____, am totally enough for my partner in our lovemaking.
13. My partner is totally enough for me in our lovemaking.
14. We only make love when both of us are in the mood.
15. Sacrifice no longer exists in our thoughts about great sex.
16. Both of us are mutually fulfilled and pleased in all our acts of lovemaking.
17. We let Joy guide us in our sex-life.

18. All that I give my partner in sex comes back to me increased in Joy and satisfaction for myself.
19. We always have the perfect environment for love making.
20. The music in our lovemaking is agreeable to both of us.
21. Our Holiness is the biggest part of sexual pleasure for us.
22. We give thanks to God for our increased pleasure and joy in Sacred Sex.

Erotic Accoutrements

The internet has changed everything. Who would have thought in 1976 when I published *I Deserve Love* we would be able to video conference friends in New Zealand for free, and see them clear as day in present time? That was futuristic *George Jetsun* stuff. Now we have Uber and WhatsApp and Dropbox at our fingertips, and Facebook and Twitter and Instagram draw us into the greatest communication tools of all time. The Social Media revolution is upon us. Keep up, or well—lag far, far behind. The nature of human communications has changed, but the subject to be communicated remains the same urgent message we all were trying to get across in 1976: "Give Peace a Chance," and when we do, "All You Need is Love!" We have seen the greatest revolution in the area of the written and spoken word since the Gutenberg press.

You can watch anything you want on YouTube. No longer can only three network TV stations dictate to you what you can or can't watch. Unlimited possibilities are at your programming fingertips, even in your sex life. What had been deemed as "pornography" in the 20th century has now become a venue for all kinds of sexual satisfactions of all shapes and sizes for all kinds of preferences. Erotic videos are one or two "clicks" away, and some of them are actually an enhancement to your sex life. Some of what we called pornography in the past is beautiful. A lot is not; a lot is like anything else appealing to our lower nature, and on the dark side of our own misplaced desire to get stimulated and feel alive any which way we can, no matter who we exploit. Maybe we are now ready to see the sexual revolution in a different light. Which is more pornographic: two lovers mutually engaged in a beautiful act of sexual pleasure, or people getting blown up and limbs severed off in some of the most violent movies of all time? Billions of dollars are invested and made in both camps.

Apps like Tinder are already known for quick hookups, mostly for the purpose of meeting up for sex with someone who turns you on but who does not make relationship demands for long term commitment. Nancy Jo Sales writes in Vanity Fair:

> *Mobile dating went mainstream about five years ago; by 2012 it was overtaking online dating. In February, one study reported there were nearly 100 million people—perhaps 50 million on Tinder alone—using their phones as a sort of all-day, every-day, handheld singles club, where they might find a sex partner as easily as they'd find a cheap flight to Florida. "It's like ordering Seamless," says Dan, the investment banker, referring to the online food-delivery service. "But you're ordering a person."*

This is also related to consumption of erotic videos on popular websites. Journalist Curtiss Silver reports this in Forbes Magazine:

It's impossible to ignore the top-level stat: that Pornhub averaged 81 million visitors per day (28.5 billion visitors for the year), with 24.7 billion searches performed. That's 50,000 searches per minute, 800 per second. The global community was active as well, with over four million videos totaling 595,492 hours uploaded. If you were to watch that much porn in a continuous fashion, your eyes would be locked onto the screen for 68 years. Don't consider that a challenge, there will probably be just as much porn uploaded this year as well.

In the area of sex toys, the largest retailer in the world, Lovehoney®, has this to say on their sales study page:

These days, sex toys are a pretty big deal - and we're not just talking about the dimensions. Some estimates place the global market for adult pleasure products at a whopping $15 billion a year - over half that of the entire US publishing industry in 2015.

Are these facts just a trend that indicate we are more widely accepting of sex as a recreational pleasure? Do they indicate that the sexual revolution has destigmatized the casual engagement of sex as though it were like any other consumable pleasure that makes us feel good? Or, as some may argue, are these trends more indicative of an underlying social and sexual malaise?

We are not here to judge, but just to point out the status quo. As for Markus and I, we support long term monogamy in which a couple is together for the evolution of their souls. Although "hookup" apps like Tinder and Friend Finder make it easy for us to find a sex partner in minutes, have we lowered ourselves to mere body sensations and not considered it is a human being with whom we are hooking up with? I Deserve Love, and that includes a deeper Spiritual Connection that uplifts me beyond the level of the body, while enjoying the pleasures of the body.

The erotic accoutrements, like any other tools of enhancement, all depend how you use them. We have sometimes explored erotic films, sex toys, and looked at the hookup apps that are out there, but in the end we are content in the simplicity of our just plain lovemaking. Our presence for each other is enough. So when we do use erotic enhancements, they are just icing on the cake, so to speak. If we were on a desert island where they did not exist, we would still have a great and fun sex life together.

The rule of thumb here is to make sure your sex-life is already well grounded and satisfying, regardless of external enhancements. How you relax into one another is far more important than how you perform and stimulate one another. For sex to approach Love you have to be spiritually aligned as well as physically aligned. If you see sex as merely a physical satisfaction, just another pleasure in your treasure trove of pleasures, just another hookup in a long series of hookups, then you will eventually fall into a meaningless search for happiness that is bound to disappoint you in the end.

Back in the sixties and seventies we had a saying— "sex and drugs and rock-and-roll," which consumed a lot of people in the hippie generation. Now we are in the Facebook and Tinder generation, and we are still allowing ourselves to be consumed. To what end? I Deserve Love first and foremost. And then, if these tools for erotic enhancement can add to that Love I already have, then all power to them. But standing by themselves, erotic accoutrements, sex toys and porn videos, hookup apps and cavalier practices of casual sex and no commitments, will only pretend to fulfill our deeper desires. What you really want with your mate is deep connection, great communication of which sex is a part, and spiritual intimacy in which you both know you are in this relationship to evolve your life purpose and your souls. Then the "main dress" for your sex-life will be the gown and glory of your most sacred union. After that, any erotic accessories will add, not subtract, to your wardrobe in the sex-life of Spiritual Intimacy.

Affirmations on Erotic Accoutrements

1. I, _____, place Love in the first place of my sex-life, and all things added after that are holy enhancements.
2. I use social media to really connect from the heart with people, especially with my lover.
3. I, _____, am clear that I love myself, and the person I am having sex with.
4. All the erotic accoutrements I use are holy and good.
5. I can accessorize and enhance an already great sex life with the toys I so desire.
6. My mate and I use erotic videos to enhance our own eroticism with each other.
7. Watching erotic videos is innocent, and I can appreciate the people who make them are innocent as well.

8. I, _____, remain balanced in my sex life, and know when I am using "sex as an outlet" to avoid something.

9. I can use Tinder to find a sex partner if I want to, and I also am willing to fully connect with this partner.

10. Sex toys are fun when I use them to add to my Joy that is already there in sex.

LGBT

Lesbian, Gay, Bisexual, and Transgender. Notice how you feel when you look at and think about those names and labels. Love is beyond a label, yet people in the 21st century do have different sexual preferences. I am not here to argue whether these are choices, reactions, biological pre-dispositions, conditioning, rebellions, obsessions, deviations or perversions. Some "bible thumpers" claim that God condemns homosexuality and all the other non-heterosexual preferences, and therefore these are worthy of our disdain. Some ask if God created a person as one gender, why would they go through a lot of trouble and medical procedures verging on the miraculous to change their sex? Like I said above, *I Deserve Love* applies to everyone, and this includes the LGBT community of people. They are people, God's people. And God created everyone with free will to decide just how they want to express themselves in this body life. As long as no harm is done to others, no domination over another and exploitation over another is part of that decision, then wouldn't Love be possible in the quotient of these choices? I believe so. We must be egalitarian here, as this is the mainstay of the American ideal—All men and women are

150

created equal in the eyes of God, and Love is everyone's birthright. This principle is without any exception.

I have trained many people over the years the art of Liberation Breathing / Rebirthing. And I also trained a few to present the Loving Relationships Training. One of these LRT® Trainers that I worked with is KW from Atlanta. I asked her if she would contribute to *I Deserve Love* with an overview of coming into her power as a lesbian woman. She has been in a monogamous relationship with her mate for 32 years. And they have been living the lifestyle of their dreams in a Loving Relationship that also has a spiritual purpose behind it. I would say they embody Spiritual Intimacy, which, in our book, is the highest calling for any Relationship. They are together for the evolution of their souls, and they know it. This is what KW writes about her life decision to be a lesbian:

> *Thank you Sondra for the opportunity to contribute to, **I Deserve Love**. It is an honor to share my overview of coming into my power as a Lesbian Woman.*
>
> *The truth is, I am really not a person who identifies through labels and roles. I never have been. I have always felt very natural in choosing females as my partners. I was raised in a very stable, healthy family and my parents are still married 50 plus years. They are very accepting and treat me lovingly. I grew up with a lot of gay friends in school. That was a real gift because we had a community we could connect with when it wasn't so popular. In my career I mostly worked with guys. That was a pleasure and I love men very much. I feel balanced in my sexuality today as a result.*

My present partner and I have been together 32 years. Our lifestyle is natural, balanced and peaceful. We have grown up together spiritually, emotionally and physically. We relate to a Holy Relationship; two full cups come together for a higher purpose. We are super independent and very much in love. We aren't threatened by space and time. We are able to be real with each other and honest. We like many of the same things and experiences so we are very busy living life to the fullest. She is my best friend, lover and companion, yet we are careful to remember that we also have individual missions to journey as well. Freedom with each other to grow individually compliments our continued desire to grow in partnership together.

When I was in training to be an LRT Trainer in the early 90's, I was the only gay person to make trainer so my teachers were very tough on me as they were concerned what my unconscious mind may attract in the audience if I was not clear. I was given many questions to answer along with assignments. It was very enlightening while my ego wanted to leave. I stuck with it and made it through to the other side much clearer. Even though being gay felt natural, the trainers were sure I was straight—so doing the inside work allowed me to be more open and innocent without hiding my true sexual preference in fear of being ridiculed. I thank you Sondra and my teachers for that gift. Leading the LRT Trainings for 24 plus years has been absolutely one of the GREATEST highlights of my life. I am forever grateful for the joy it continues to bring me and others, straight and gay.

In closing, for me, Pure Love is infinite and beyond limitations no matter what the sexual identification. It cannot be harmed, broken, crushed or destroyed. Whether the form is male or female, the content is Love. If there is confusion, that can be processed and worked through. I recommend forgiveness on self and others to stay clear and innocent if there is any doubt. We all deserve authentic love and pleasure. We don't have to prove anything or overcompensate. We are all people of worth and children of God.
—KW of Atlanta

Affirmations on Being Lesbian from KW

1. I love myself exactly as I am.
2. My sexuality is innocent.
3. I am just right for me.
4. I deserve to be happy and loved.
5. I have something special to offer.
6. I am just right as a lesbian woman.
7. I love and approve of myself.
8. I am free to be me.
9. I draw from my inner strength and light.
10. I choose to see the light that I am to this world.
11. I am deeply fulfilled with who I am.

Being gay in 2019 is probably easier than in 1976 when I first wrote this book on deserving Love. Most of my clients then were young women who were coming to me with all their relationship problems, sexual problems, and family problems. Everybody has some of those. But when I started teaching the Loving Relationships Training, it attracted many gay men. When I asked my gay friends about the LRT®, and did it all apply to them too, they said, "Sure Sondra, we have the same issues with love, commitment, overcoming our "personal lies," getting over our family patterns that everyone else has. It is right on, in our world." So I felt good at the time that the main training I created to help people transform and evolve applied to gay people as well.

CB is one of my gay friends in Florida who took the LRT many years ago. Now he is an MD having put himself through medical school. He has this to say about how the principles he learned in the LRT weekend seminar, and those of Rebirthing transformed his life and helped him come into his power being gay—and following his dreams to become a doctor:

> Hello Dear Reader, I consider myself fortunate to have discovered the principles of rebirthing and the LRT week-end seminar. I have always had the desire to help others in whatever way I could, and I believe this desire has led me to the path of becoming a doctor. I love having a career which is based on helping others discover optimal levels of health and well-being. Before I could achieve this goal I had to to challenge my own "personal lie" of "not being good enough." How could I help anyone if I didn't think I was even "good enough" to do so? The LRT has been instrumental in the way I have reframed my thinking about myself and what I am capable of

accomplishing. God created me more than good enough! The LRT training also facilitated the loving relationship I have with the Creator, Father-Mother God. There is an entire section in the LRT devoted to creating greater clarity over any toxic religious beliefs that cloud our perception of how beautiful and perfect we really are.

I was raised in a religious household and taught to believe that homosexuality was punishable by eternal damnation. This should offer a huge conflict for anyone who believes in a loving God and especially if that someone is gay. Now that I know that the Universe itself is on my side I can allow myself to have healthier and more loving relationships, and to create the mag-nificent life I am constantly re-inventing. Affirmations are a part of this magical journey. Below are a few affirmations that I have included for anyone creating greater self-love, self-discovery and desiring to smooth out some of the bumps we all experience on this journey we call Life.

—CB of South Florida

Affirmations on Being Gay from CB

1. I am created by the Father-Mother God who is perfect. That which is perfect can only create perfection therefore I am perfect as I am.
2. I am enough, I do enough, I have enough.
3. The Universe itself wants me to succeed.
4. The love I desire is already made manifest.
5. I am safe. I am safe to love, I am safe to grow, I am safe to be who I am.

6. Life is good. Everything in my life is ultimately here to allow me to grow.
7. With every breath I take I am better and better in every way.
8. I choose my life because, well—there is no because—I simply choose my life.
9. I love and accept myself.
10. I am in the right place at the right time engaged in the right activity with the right people.

Another Gay friend of ours in Florida, Dr. Bob Walsh, who has taken the LRT® many times from me, has this to say about how the training and breathwork has helped him in his life:

> *The Loving Relationships Training is all about relationships—and the most important relationship is the one with ourselves. With the skills I learned in the training, and still use to this day, I have had successful relationships for the past 30 years. Even when the relationship ends, or I should say changes, we both feel peaceful and good about our time together.*
>
> *Being gay, we still have the same relationship issues that everyone else does, but we also have social, religious, family and other issues. Depending on the part of the country you are in, and it can be different for different people, the LRT gave me the most spiritual relationship I have today—the one with myself. This one is transferred to all relationships in my life, including family, friends, patients and community. It allowed me to come out as a professional gay man when very few*

had the courage to step out. And it gave me the strength and tools to be who I am, and live my life to the fullest. It was a powerful training, and combined with the breathing techniques that I also use in my daily life today, it gave me a very good quality of life. I am sincerely grateful for Sondra Ray, the LRT, and Rebirthing / Breathwork for all it has given me and the world at large.
Dr. Bob Walsh—South Florida

Affirmations from Dr. Bob Walsh

1. I am free to be who I am.
2. The more I am fully me, the more I am loved and accepted as me.
3. I appreciate all of me.
4. I accept myself and my sexuality as an expression of my Divinity.
5. My sexuality is a beautiful part of me.
6. People enjoy and connect with me more when I am completely me.
7. It is safe to be who I am.
8. My relationships are as fulfilling as I allow them to be.
9. Accepting myself in a predominantly heterosexual culture is an ongoing process.
10. My family are those who love and accept me for who I am.

We met AG from Perth who is a Chiropractor. She had sessions with us to get over the guilt she felt for some former abuse she had as a child. And also, we found out, she was a healer in a past life around the time of King

157

James I in England, and she was accused of being a witch and probably burned at the stake. This was a powerful session, and she let go of a lot of guilt and shame and feelings of powerlessness. In fact, she is a very powerful woman in this life, and very serious about her work as a healer/Chiropractor to serve others.

Her last intimate relationship was with a woman, but now she is currently single and healing herself of all past relationships that did not work out. She has been with guys as well. This is what she says about being bi-sexual:

> *Being bisexual wasn't a conscious decision that I woke up and made one day. It's not like waking up and deciding what color shoes to wear with your outfit. Sexuality doesn't work that way.*
>
> *Growing up, I didn't identify with being gay, however, I didn't identify with being heterosexual either. I was just myself, trying to come to terms with a bit of a traumatic past. My first sexual experiences were non-consenting acts at the hands of two of my uncles. I had to do a lot of healing work to learn to express sexuality with love, the way that I'm sure the Goddess intended humans to do so.*
>
> *I was in my twenties when I realized that I could connect with women just as easily as I could with men. At first I was concerned that I was avoiding relationships with males because of my sexual abuse. But as I continued to heal myself emotionally, I realized that my bisexuality was a healthy and normal part of me. I came to understand that it is a part of me that deserves loving expression, like any other aspect of my consciousness. What a wonderful gift it is, to be*

able to form intimate connections with both men & women. To be bisexual is to have an ability to see beyond gender and labels & fall in love with the energetic being behind the physical body.

Affirmations on Being Bisexual from AG

1. I am as God / the Goddess created me.
2. I am Love.
3. Sex is healing.
4. I honor the divine masculine within me.
5. I honor the divine feminine within me.
6. I am Love all of the time.
7. Sex is holy.
8. My sexuality flows easily.
9. My heart is open.
10. I, _____, deserve Love from myself, from a woman, or from a man.

The most touching experience we have had with the LGBTQ community was with Nikolas Gripp in Glastonbury, England, at a 9-day training on Liberation Breathing and Physical Immortality. I shared a little earlier that when I went into his room to assist him and his Rebirther, I immediately felt like a huge stuck energy. I asked him about his "sex life," and he began to share—it all came out. He was a girl and now he is a man. This was the first transgender man I had in a training, and I was really glad about it.

There was so much healing and acceptance that took place for him during the training. He totally "came out," so to speak, and we were all so privileged to be part of his transformation. He was beginning to see that his role would be to become a Rebirther for others who also grappled with their gender. He would serve those who either wanted to go through a sex change, were in the process of it, or had already gone through it like himself. All this was so enlightening for us in the training. We were all given the opportunity to accept and be loving to another for decisions he made about sex with which we were not too familiar. Nikolas has this to say about his process of becoming a man:

I was 4.5 years old when I told my mother that I did not want to continue going to pre-school because I didn't want to wear the uniform. The uniform I was expected to wear was a dress. I was never able to connect or accept my female body nor did I ever identify as a "girl."

Growing up in the 80s there was not much talk about transgender people where I lived, so I grew up feeling gender neutral. But I knew something was off. I started self-harming at a very young age and I never really had a desire to live.

Once I found out that I had the option to transition I started living full time as a man. I used to bind my chest, work at jobs that didn't require showing ID and hoped that nobody would ever find out. Every person in my life that I was close to rejected me, but I had to keep strong because I had a long challenging road in front of me when I decided to actually change my sex!

I had to raise thousands of Euros to pay for all the surgeries and also make sure that I was sane enough to face a world that thought I was a freak. I was open about being transgender before my transition because I wanted others to start accepting transgender people. Once I was done with my surgeries and had legally changed my name and gender, I was so drained psychologically that I kept it to myself. I just wanted to live a normal life, like a normal man.

And I knew that by doing so I was rejecting my journey, my past, but I honestly couldn't handle anything more at the time. After 10 years of silence I started training as a Breathwork Practitioner and psychologically preparing myself to live an open life as a transgender man.

When Sondra Ray came into the room as I was doing a breathwork session and started asking me questions, I thought, "It's now or never." Sondra encouraged me to be open about being transgender during the training, so I decided to share it with the whole group. I received a lot of Love and Acceptance from everyone. It was overwhelming.

I always felt less of a man, as if I didn't have the right to call myself a man. Breathwork has helped me enormously. I have been able to clear a lot of trauma that was stored in my body. And it also helped me to build my confidence and to feel more comfortable with whom I am.

—Nikolas Gripp of London, UK

Affirmations on Being Transgender by Nikolas Gripp

1. I deserve to be loved for being exactly who I am.
2. I am now attracting people in my life who are willing to fully accept me for who I am.

3. I deserve to live the life of my choice, free and full of love.
4. I accept myself completely.
5. I am worthy and deserving of love and acceptance.
6. We are both masculine and feminine. Every side of me deserves my love.
7. I am proud of myself for being brave enough to live as a transgender man.
8. I love, appreciate and accept my body.
9. When I accept myself, others will accept me.
10. It's safe to be myself.

The Rainbow Millennium is upon us. I Deserve Love acknowledges that all deserve love, no matter what their sexual preferences are. We have all been created by the Divine, and we have to come to a place inside of ourselves that is free of judgments and opinions about others who may have different orientations around sex than we do.

I thank my friends above for contributing to this important chapter on the LGBTQ community. We join hands in this rainbow of multi-colored members, and celebrate our diversity, rather than judge our differences. There is a wonderful lesson in A Course in Miracles that says, "Let me perceive no differences today." (Lesson 262) Well, when we have truly applied this lesson, we will see with the eyes of tolerance and peace, and embrace everyone, no matter what their sexual preference, in the group hug of 7.5 billion human members, seeing finally the gloriousness of our divine and diverse spectrum of rainbow colors.

Epilogue

My present work is more exciting than ever; and I must say that I have never seen anything yet that produces such dramatic results for people! What I am referring to is Rebirthing, which we now call Liberation Breathing®, the Divine Mother's Gift, combined with The Loving Relationships Training. Leonard Orr conceived the Rebirthing Process way back in 1973, and I wish everyone could do it. What we do is simulate the process of birth and provide a way of eliminating from consciousness the negative effects of one's birth trauma. This is done in the presence of someone who has already gone through the process, and released his or her own past traumas. This conscious connected *energy breathing* can be done lying down flat on your back, or curled up in a fetal position under water, breathing through a snorkel! (the wet method with a snorkel takes considerable preparation). It took me quite awhile to become a really good "Rebirther," because of the clarity and intuitiveness required. The number one requirement, however, is that the Rebirther must have his or her own birth trauma worked out, which provides others a feeling of safety and helps them to be willing to let the memory of their own birth come up to consciousness. The results are fantastic. When I see someone get on the other side of it, into a state of bliss (wherein they often tell me they have never felt so good in their entire life), I feel at those

163

moments that there is no place in the world I would rather be. The joy that fills the room is so intense that I often weep. I see it as one of the best forms of preventive medicine and sex therapy I have yet encountered.

Sondra Ray

About the Authors

SONDRA RAY, author of 23 books on the subjects of relationships, healing, and spiritual matters, was launched into international acclaim in the 1970s as one of the pioneers, along with Leonard Orr, of the Rebirthing Experience. She has trained thousands of people all over the world in this conscious connected breathing process, and is considered one of the foremost experts on how the birth trauma affects one's body, relationships, career and life. As she puts it, "This dynamic breathing process produces extraordinary healing results in all of your relationships—with your mate, with yourself and with Life—very fast. By taking in more Life Force through the breath, limiting thoughts and memories, which are the cause of all problems and disease, come to the surface of the mind so they can be 'breathed out', forgiven and released."

Applying over 40 years of metaphysical study, she has helped thousands of people heal their negative thought structures, birth trauma, habitual family patterns and unconscious death urge, which have affected their life. She encourages people to make lasting positive changes through Liberation Breathing® to be more free, happy and productive. No matter what Sondra Ray is doing, she is always trying to bring about a higher consciousness. Recently she has written two new books on the subject of *Spiritual Intimacy©* and *BABAJI: My Miraculous Meetings with a Maha Avatar*, which she envisions will shift the current paradigm in relationships around the world to a new level of consciousness—free from anger and conflict. She has also written *Physical Immortality: How to Overcome Death*. This book is destined to liberate people from their unconscious acceptance that "death" and aging just happen to us, apart from our consciousness.

MARKUS RAY, artist, poet, and twin flame of Sondra Ray, received his training in the arts, holding degrees from the Cleveland Institute of Art, And Tyler School of Art of Temple University in Philadelphia. He is the author of a major work, Odes to the Divine Mother, which contains 365 prose poems in praise of the Divine Feminine Energy. Along with the Odes are his paintings and images of the Divine Mother created around the world in his mission with Sondra Ray.

Markus is a presenter of the profound modern psychological/spiritual scripture, A Course in Miracles. He studied with his master, Tara Singh, for 17 years, in order to experience its truth directly. His spiritual quest has taken him to India many times with Tara Singh and Sondra Ray, where Muniraj, Babaji's foremost disciple, gave him the name Man Mohan, "The Poet who steals the hearts of the people". In all of his paintings, writings and lectures, Markus creates a quiet atmosphere of peace and clarity that is an invitation to go deeper into the realms of inner stillness, silence and beauty. He teaches, writes and paints along-side of Sondra Ray, and many have been touched by their demonstration of a holy relationship in action. His iconic paintings of the Masters can be viewed on markusray.com which he often creates while his twin flame, Sondra Ray, is lecturing in seminars.

Other Books by
SONDRA RAY & MARKUS RAY

❖ **I DESERVE LOVE**

Sondra shows you how to use affirmations to achieve goals in love, life, and sexual pleasure.

❖ **CELEBRATION OF BREATH**

A discussion of the basic steps we can all take to produce well-being, physical perfection, and longevity.

❖ **THE ONLY DIET THERE IS**

You can create the physical being you want by using the incredible power of the mind to transform attitudes about eating.

❖ **LOVING RELATIONSHIPS**

How to find, achieve, and maintain a deeper, more fulfilling relationship.

❖ **IDEAL BIRTH**

How to create a conscious and enlightened conception, pregnancy, and delivery. Now in its Second Edition.

❖ **DRINKING THE DIVINE**

This is Sondra's own exploration of her experience and use of the spiritual work, A Course in Miracles.

❖ REBIRTHING IN THE NEW AGE
Co-authored with Leonard Orr, this is an in-depth look at the way to create perfect health, effortless bliss, prosperity, perpetual youth, and Immortality.

❖ BIRTH & RELATIONSHIPS
Co-authored with Bob Mandel, this book shows you how the type of birth you had (cesarean, breech, forceps, "regular") affects your personality.

❖ PURE JOY
Sondra shares her discoveries of the many spiritual practices we can use to find pure joy in our lives.

❖ HOW TO BE CHIC, FABULOUS AND LIVE FOREVER
Sondra explores in depth the possibilities and realities of Physical Immortality; with contributions by other Immortalists.

❖ INNER COMMUNION
Sondra goes to Yugoslavia to meet the children who are having apparitions of the Virgin Mary.

❖ INTERLUDES WITH THE GODS
Sondra gives her account of meeting with remarkable spiritual Masters who have shaped and influenced her life and teaching.

❖ LOVING RELATIONSHIPS II
This is the sequel to the very popular Loving Relationships book that describes the principles to having great relationships.

❖ THE LOVING RELATIONSHIPS TREASURY
A compendium of the wisdom of Sondra Ray when it comes to creating and clearing lasting relationships

❖ HEALING AND HOLINESS
Sondra describes what she went through in experiencing the "dark night of the soul," and how she came out of it.

❖ PELE'S WISH
This is a concise account of the wisdom and teachings of the Hawaiian Spiritual Masters.

❖ ROCK YOUR WORLD WITH THE DIVINE MOTHER
This book is a Westerners guide to understanding the Divine Feminine concept of God in a mostly patriarchal, male oriented context.

❖ LIBERATION BREATHING: THE DIVINE MOTHER'S GIFT
Sondra wrote her classic "Bible on Breathwork," and this is it.

❖ SPIRITUAL INTIMACY: WHAT YOU REALLY WANT WITH A MATE
Co-authored with her husband, Markus Ray, this is a new guide to a spiritual partnership in which a couple's divine practice and destiny together is emphasized kept in the forefront.

❖ BABAJI: MY MIRACULOUS MEETINGS WITH A MAHA AVATAR
Co-Authored with her husband, this is a eyewitness account by Sondra of her meetings and teachings received from the modern Maha Avatar Babaji in India and beyond. It also contains Markus's paintings and verse in homage to Babaji.

❖ THE NEW LOVING RELATIONSHIPS BOOK
Co-Authored with her husband, this is a 2nd edition of the popular Loving Relationships title, rewritten for these times.

❖ PHYSICAL IMMORTALITY: HOW TO OVERCOME DEATH
Sondra Ray co-authors with her husband to present a manual for overcoming the "unconscious death urge"—our subconscious thoughts and beliefs that contribute to aging and death. Life extension and the Immortalist Life Style are also the themes discussed.

❖ ODES TO THE DIVINE MOTHER
365 Odes to The Divine Mother scribed by Markus Ray in setting around the world give people a deeper insight into the Divine Mother in Everyday life. Intro by Sondra.

❖ MIRACLES WITH MY MASTER, TARA SINGH: APPLICATIONS OF A COURSE IN MIRACLES
Markus describes his 17 years studying with A Course in Miracles teacher, Tara Singh, and the applications of miracles in his life as a result of this holy relationship.

❖ THE MASTER IS BEAUTIFUL
This description of nine spiritual Masters can enlighten anyone's concept of gurus and teachers who have swayed the evolution of the human soul for the better. Markus presents nine spiritual Masters who have influenced his own spiritual awakening, and who can also affect yours.

Find Sondra Ray & Markus Ray on
Amazon.com

SONDRA RAY'S Author's Portal :

Bit.ly/SondraRay

MARKUS RAY'S Author's Portal :

Bit.ly/MarkusRay

Other Resources

Sondra Ray / author, teacher, Rebirther, creator of the Loving
Relationships Training®, Founder of Liberation Breathing®
Facebook: www.facebook.com/sondra.ray.90
Facebook Fan Page: www.facebook.com/LiberationBreathing
Twitter: www.twitter.com/SondraRay1008
YouTube: www.youtube.com/SondraRay
Website: www.sondraray.com

Markus Ray / poet, author, artist, Rebirther, presenter of *A
Course in Miracles*, Co-founder of Liberation Breathing®
Facebook: www.facebook.com/markus.ray.169
Facebook Fan Page: www.facebook.com/LiberationBreathing
Twitter: www.twitter.com/MarkusRay1008
Website: www.markusray.com
"Art Look" – an art lovers companion – www.markusray.com

301 Tingey Street, SE, #338, Washington D.C. 20003
E-mail: contact@sondraray.com
E-mail: contact@markusray.com

Babaji and The Divine Mother Resources:

Babaji's Ashram in Haidakhan (India)
E-mail: info@haidakhanbabaji.com

Haidakhandi Samaj (India)
E-mail: Info@HaidakhandiSamaj.org

See Sondra Ray & Markus Ray on these Websites:

www.sondraray.com   and   www.markusray.com

www.facebook.com/LiberationBreathing

We encourage you, our reader, to attend The Loving Relationships Training (The LRT®) which is produced by Immortal Ray Productions all over the world. You can see Sondra Ray & Markus Ray's worldwide teaching schedule on www.sondraray.com/programs-seminars/

Also, we encourage you to attend The INDIA QUEST, The BALI QUEST, or other Spiritual Quests that teach and disseminate Liberation Breathing practices, and principles of A Course in Miracles, as well as enhance your Divine Connection to various Spiritual Masters. These are also available on www.sondraray.com

Artwork and paintings of the Spiritual Masters by Markus Ray are available on www.markusray.com

Liberation Breathing   Book a Session at   bit.ly/LBSession

Join us on an International Quest

DEC. 3 — DEC 13 — EVERY YEAR

RETURN TO THE DIVINE MOTHER IN BALI, THE ISLAND OF THE GODS, AND THE WORSHIP OF THE SACRED FEMININE !

Join SONDRA RAY on her BALI QUEST , an exquisite journey of the soul to this ancient holy culture.

BALI
QUEST with SONDRA RAY

ARRIVE: DEC 3
DEPART: DEC 13
EVERY YEAR

◆ **JOIN SONDRA RAY** in this life changing event. Journey to **BALI,** one of the most special places on the planet. Discover your sacred Self at most holy **Besakih Mother Temple.**

◆ Pay homage to the Divine Mother of all LIFE in BALI, and usher in 2019 at one of the

"Immortality Power Points". Stretch your mind and open your heart on this profound journey. Visit the sacred waters of **Pura Tirta Empul Temple.**

◆ Arrive in Bali on DEC 3rd and meet the "Mother of Rebirthing", **SONDRA RAY,** to begin this quest of spiritual awakening through **Liberation Breathing®** from the Divine Mother. Witness **Gamelan Music & Balinese Dancing.** Soak up the rich Balinese culture that for centuries has worshipped the Divine Mother in practices of unrivaled beauty and grace.

◆ Total cost of the Bali Quest is $3500 US. ($3000 for Early Reg. Before Sept 1.) This includes transfers to the beautiful **Nefatari Villas of Ubud,** double and quad villa occupancy in traditional Balinese settings, Balinese cuisine, some planned excursions, and Bali Quest training tuition.

◆ **Register Here**: https://sondraray.com/programs-quests/

◆ Only 25 Spaces available.

◆ Email <contact@sondraray.com> for info and program.

Contact: <contact@sondraray.com> or MARKUS RAY at <manmohan1008@gmail.com>

For more info on SONDRA RAY : < https://sondraray.com/ >

174

Notes

Notes